<u>PATRISTIC MONOGRAPH SERIES, NO. 4</u>

WITHDRAWN

GOD THE ANONYMOUS

A Study in

Alexandrian Philosophical Theology

by

Joseph C. McLelland

Published by

The Philadelphia Patristic Foundation, Ltd.

1976

... it was Alexandria that gave rise
to Christian Hellenism, which was to
become the miracle of human history.

-Jean Daniélou

The unfading merit of Clement and Origen
is that they created the Christian
philosophy. This *philosophia perennis*
is Christian Platonism ...

-Einar Molland

... the wondrous name, above all names,
the anonymous ...

-Denis the Areopagite

i

CONTENTS

P R E F A C E

The roots of Western thought lie buried in Greek soil, but they were tended and nourished by Jews and Christians who introduced something new: a feeling for history, a sense of timing. The convergence of two distinct streams produced, in theological terms, "classical theism" or "Christian Hellenism." Our thesis is that the Alexandrian philosophical theology (or religious philosophy), represented by Philo, Clement and Origen, expresses the greatness as well as the ambiguity of that convergence. It has been the subject of much debate, put most strongly by Harnack's charge that "Origen transformed the whole content of ecclesiastical faith into ideas" through his idealistic philosophy. It is significant, too, that attitudes toward the Alexandrians vary from the positive appreciation of Roman and Anglican to more critical and even hostile reception among Reformed scholars (the article by W.H. Wagner is helpful in this regard). Such variation is part of the sociology of knowledge, no doubt, but serves to remind us how complex our topic is as to interpretation and relevance for contemporary theology.

This work reflects the conviction that the modern dilemma over theological method and agenda is, in large part, the result of misunderstanding "the roots of Western thought." Either we take for granted our classical heritage and so underestimate its power, or we neglect its wisdom and flounder in a less adequate problematic devised solely by "modernity." In either case a return to sources may help orient our situation and show how to "overcome theology by theology."

A process of reflection on the discipline called "philosophy of religion" lies behind the work. Engaged in this enterprise for twenty years, I see a constant need to confront my students and myself with

iv

the heritage of classical theism, but also with the fact of its breakdown for modern man and the need to construct viable alternatives. My *thesis* is stated in the first and last chapters, with the three chapters on the Alexandrians as a sort of case study, the analytic for the thesis. The final sections ('Classical Theism and the Crucified God' and 'A Name for God') form a programmatic essay suggestive of the way I see today's theological project. It reflects my current research, in which the curious influence of the Prometheus myth since the Enlightenment convinces me that classical theism encouraged Western man to cast God in the role of Zeus, interpreted as aloof and impassive (Lucky's famous speech in *Waiting for Godot* is a precious parody of what theologians sound like!). Hence the need to play a Promethean part, accepting responsibility, especially for the problem of evil. The project is phrased in terms borrowed from Paul Ricoeur and others; this does not pretend that there is a "system" ready and waiting; only a proper concern for right interpretation, a hermeneutic appropriate to the data.

An initial draft of this book received a prize from the Christian Research Foundation (1959-60). Many experts have been consulted along the way. Three colleagues deserve mention and an expression of my gratitude. Wilfred Cantwell Smith encouraged my early research; Raymond Klibansky's remarkable historical knowledge has proved most stimulating. Eric Jay, with whom I shared a graduate seminar on Origen, has read this volume diligently--I offer him my thanks and note that whatever errors in style or judgment remain are my own. The typescript was prepared by Virginia Bryce. To my wife I owe continuing gratitude for her support and understanding in my research and writing avocation.

J.C. McLelland

S I G L A

(1) ABBREVIATIONS

ACW   Ancient Christian Writers. Westminster, Md.,
and London, 1946ff

ANL   Ante-Nicene Christian Library. Edinburgh,
1864ff

EP   Encyclopedia of Philosophy. 8 vols. N.Y.:
Macmillan, 1967

GCS   Die griechischen christlichen Schriftsteller
der ersten drei Jahrhunderte. Berlin,
1897ff

HTR   Harvard Theological Review

JTS   Journal of Theological Studies

LCC   Library of Christian Classics. London:
SCM, 1953-

NPNF   Library of Nicene and Post-Nicene Fathers.
Second Series. Oxford and N.Y., 1890ff

PG   Patrologia graeca, J-P Migne, 1 - 161.
Paris, 1857-1866

SC   Collection 'Sources Chrétiennes.' Paris,
1942-

SJT   Scottish Journal of Theology

Philo

Abr.	De Abrahamo
Aet.	De aeternitate mundi
Cher.	De Cherubim
Conf.	De confusione linguarum
Det.	Quod deterius potiori insidiari soleat
Fug.	De fuga et inventione
Immut.	Quod Deus sit immutabilis
Leg. All.	Legum allegoriae
Migr.	De migratione Abrahae
Mut.	De mutatione nominum
Opif.	De opificio mundi
Plant.	De plantatione Noe
Post. C.	De posteritate Caini
Praem.	De praemiis et poenis
Prov.	De providentia
Qu. Gen.	Quaestiones in Genesim
Quis Rer.	Quis rerum divinarum heres sit
Sacr.	De sacrificiis Abelis et Caini
Somn.	De somniis
Virt.	De virtutibus
V. contempl.	De vita contemplativa
V. Mos.	De vita Mosis

Clement

Ecl. Proph.	Eclogae propheticae
Paed.	Paedagogus
Prot.	Protrepticus
Q.D.S.	Quis dives salvetur?
Str.	Stromateis
Exc.	Excerpta ex Theodoto

C. Cels.	Contra Celsum
De Orat.	De Oratione
De Princ.	De principiis
Dial. Herac.	Dialogue with Heraclides
Exh. mart.	Exhortatio ad martyrium
Hom. Gen., etc.	Homiliae in Genesim, etc.
In Matt., etc.	Commentarium in Evangelium Matthaei, etc.

References: *Str.* vi.XII.104.3 refers to book six of the *Stromateis*, chapter twelve in the ANF text and section 104.3 in GCS.

(2) TEXTS AND EDITIONS

Philo: Loeb Classical Library, 12 vols. 1950ff; trans. Colson and Whitaker

Clement: GCS 12,15,17,39, ed. Otto Stählin. Leipzig, 1905-1936
SC 2,23,30,38,70,108,158

Origen: GCS 2,3,6,10,22,29,30,33,35,38,40,41, ed. P. Koetschau etc., Leipzig, 1899-1941
SC 7,16,29,37,67,71,87,120,132,136,147,150, 157,162

Origen on First Principles, G.W. Butterworth (trans. of Koetschau text), N.Y.: Harper and Row 1966

Contra Celsum, Henry Chadwick (trans. of Koetschau text), Cambridge 1965

Exhaustive bibliographies in CROUZEL 1961 and HARL, pp 31-68

(3) SYSTEM OF REFERENCE

The method of referring adopted is one gaining increasing favor because it eliminates footnotes and renders the Bibliography functional. All references are placed within parentheses in the body of the text. Thus (JONES: 3ff) lists author's name and the pages of his text cited in the Bibliography. If the author has more than one work listed, publication dates are used to distinguish (JONES 1962: 3ff). If more than one Jones is listed, initials are given; if more than one volume, the volume number (A.B. JONES 1962: II.3ff).

CHAPTER 1

GREEK RELIGION AND PHILOSOPHY

The central question for the Greek mind was, how can man relate to transcendent Being? Philosophy's task was "the saving of the appearances," a witness to the One behind the manifold of experience. "The problem of Platonism was to build a bridge from the many to the one" (COCHRANE: 428). Thus the finite is capable of infinity because the human mind is essentially one with divinity, sharing the immutable realm of Being. This tenet is obvious in the greatest philosophical system of Greece, Platonism; it also informs its greatest religious system, Orphism. Both sought to answer the same question, and both answers share a similarly optimistic or idealistic flavor.

This sort of "optimistic rationalism," however, is only part of the story—our traditional concentration on philosophy as a rationalistic enterprise obscures the true background of Western thought. One need not be a disciple of Heidegger to feel the point of his thesis that we are guilty of a "forgetting of being" by interpreting philosophy as rationalistic and de-mythologizing (HEIDEGGER 1962: 2). Such concentration and interpretation misses the *other* Greece, with its dualistic answer, its pessimism and anxiety.

Our thesis is that this latter element or stream in Greek thought was sidetracked by the exaltation of optimistic rationalism, first by Platonism itself and then by the Christian Platonism of the Church Fathers. The chief mark of such exaltation is a failure to do justice to the problem of evil, and to the correlative question of divine suffering. In order to develop the thesis in relation to the Alexandrian school, I shall first examine briefly the "other Greece," and then turn to the Platonist development.

1

Plato's dialogue *Euthyphro* allows Socrates to "bring forth" a critique of religion which stands as the *locus classicus* of his attitude toward popular religion. Euthyphro had defined piety and holiness as aspects of justice, that part of justice which pertains to the gods: "giving the gods their due," "a sort of therapy of the gods" which must be "of the nature of service or ministration." Prayer and sacrifice please the gods: this is the service which men do for them.

Socrates turns this definition (section 14) most aptly: "*Soc*... Now, as the asker of a question is necessarily dependent on the answerer, whither he leads I must follow; and can only ask again, what is the pious, and what is piety? Do you mean that they are a sort of science of praying and sacrificing? *Euth.* Yes, I do. *Soc.* And sacrificing is giving to the gods, and prayer is asking of the gods? *Euth.* Yes, Socrates. *Soc.* Upon this view, then, piety is a science of asking and giving? *Euth.* You understand me capitally, Socrates... *Soc.* Then piety, Euthyphro, is an art which gods and men have of doing business with one another?" Now Euthyphro dislikes this logic of his position, but can offer nothing better. He retreats from the Socratic irony-- "I am in a hurry, and must go now."

Thus religion is defined as *do ut des*, a business transaction according to the rules of divine justice which human service observes. It is a just and even kindly "therapy" or "tendance" of the gods on the part of man. Such logic fits the general Olympian religion of the classical tradition. But primitive piety itself involved a second element, probably as important as the first, and always significant. This was called *deisidaimonia*, "fear of the spirits" or better, "fear of the supernatural." It is the service of evil, rendered out of fear, in order to be rid of the threat of divine retribution. Plutarch's famous treatise *On Superstition* associated it with weakness: "the superstitious are afraid of the gods, yet fly to them for refuge, flatter and yet revile them, invoke them and yet heap blame upon them" (*De Superst.* 1 - HARRISON: 5; F.C. GRANT: 72f).

Jane Harrison has shown how *deisidaimonia* replaced the formula *do ut des* with another, *do ut abeas:* no longer do I give that you may reward, but that you may depart! Alongside the ministry proper to the Olympian deities, then, is this "aversion" proper to the alien demons of the underworld. Plato calls the latter "gods of aversion" (*Laws* 854B), while the orator Isocrates declared: "Some of the gods are mild and humane, others harsh and unpleasant... Those of the gods who are the source to us of good things have the title of Olympians, those whose department is that of calamities and punishments have harsher titles; to the first class both private persons and states erect altars and temples, the second is not worshipped either with prayers or burnt-sacrifices, but in their case we perform ceremonies of riddance" (*Or.* v.117 - HARRISON: 8).

The riddance ceremonies formed a sort of liturgy of negation similar to the detailed rites of exorcism of the medieval Church. Whereas the ritual of Olympian therapy normally involved a communion meal, this *apotropê* involves the destruction of a victim. The first requires an altar, the second a trench, leading into the underworld abode of the demons. Plato can describe the gods as "fellow guests" with men, but these darker demons are not included. The dualism remains in Greek religion, Zeus himself later including the two elements of Meilichios and Maimaktes, easily-approached and raging. Sometimes altar and trench existed side by side, or even altar, eschara (for hero-worship) and trench (cf *Laws* 717f). Plutarch speaks of "two priests, one to supervise things divine, one for the demonic."

The dualism was not maintained in a fruitful way, however, except perhaps in some mystery-cults. We suggest that there are two main streams of Greek

3

thought, corresponding in a general way to these two
elements of its religion. The darker element is ack-
nowledged in Greek tragedy and mystery; the lighter in
its "philosophical" development.

Mystery and Tragedy

        A mystery involves two sorts of secret, the
arrêton or ineffable reality, and the *aporrêton*, forbidden by the law of silence (KERENYI: 26). Or: some
things one *may* not tell, others one *can*not. He who is
initiated into the mystery is being prepared to behold
sacred things, the vision of which is not to be uttered
to the uninitiated. The initiate is first *mystês*,
then *epoptês*--having seen but forbidden to tell. The
term "mystery" is derived from both *myô*, to close the
apertures of eyes and mouth, and *myeô*, to begin or initiate (KERENYI: 46). Whether the element of ineffability is as early as that of purification or *tabu* remains a question. Jane Harrison stressed the purification as prelude to the handling of *sacra*, and defined
mystery as "a rite in which certain sacra are exhibited,
which cannot be safely seen by the worshipper till he
has undergone certain purifications" (HARRISON: 151;
but see KERENYI: 24ff).

        Our concern is not with the complex history
of the mysteries; rather, we wish to show that their
concern for purity and riddance maintains the dark
element in Greek religion already noted, and is the
historical foil for the philosophical development.
Moreover, their preoccupation with fertility through
totemistic ritual belongs to man's perennial search
for the secret of Nature and the powers of natural
immortality. In the lat e r refinements of Mithraism
and Orphism this generates a striking theology of
redemption. It indicates that "other Greece" beside
and beneath the classic philosophy which has been un-
duly isolated in modern historiography (NILSSON: 153;
but NORDEN: 113 denies the importance of "the mystic-
ecstatic element" for the Greek mind).

4

When Dionysos invaded Greece, sometime after Homer's great literary work, he was a militant deity, already adept at conquering religions of lesser power. Euripides has him say:

> And now I come to Hellas, having taught
> All the world else my dances and my rite
> Of mysteries, to show me in man's sight
> Manifest God. *(Bacch.* 13*)*

In his Bacchic form, Dionysos offered the gift *(charis)* of wine, the intoxicant by means of which the worshipper could achieve God-possession, "enthusiasm." It was this frenzied cult, originating in a bull-totemism of the cattlemen *(bykoloi)* of Asia Minor, now represented by Bacchus and Sabazios, by wild dances on mountainside and ecstatic, even drunken worship, which the gentle poet Orpheus met and conquered. This legendary hero moralized the Dionysian idea of God, and raised men's hopes to a union with the divine. The Orphic mystery preserved the ancient rites of a meal of "living flesh," of flaming torches and bodily purgation; but it re-mythologized its inheritance so that the new focus lay upon the mystic vision, sealed in sacred marriage (KIRK-RAVEN: 37ff; PETTAZZONI: 108ff; HARRISON: 454ff).

The critique levelled at the Orphic rites by Aristophanes and by Plato should not blind us to the fact that theirs was the caricature of an essentially noble mystery cult. No doubt ritual purification became degraded into formalism and legalism; Plato decries the "seers and mendicant quacks" who peddle their mysteries *(Rep.* 2.364B). Yet the heart of Orphism was its offer of redemption; the first article of its creed was, "I have flown out of the sorrowful weary Wheel." This doctrine of a reincarnational cycle was presupposed by Platonism equally with Orphism, the former substituting the power of rational thinking for that of ritual purification.

Myth and ritual, liturgies of mediation and rebirth: the Mysteries served generation after gene-

ration--Eleusis for over a millennium, so that one might
posit "an identification of Greek experience with the
Mysteries" (KERENYI: 18). The fertility motif is important, though not so decisive as reductionists such as
James Frazer once imagined. More than "a simple rustic
festival" is on view: redemption by union with the god
was not an escalation of agricultural needs, but a recognition of the human condition and its implications.
The initiates at Eleusis understood the preliminary
myths and the ritual of revelation as a victory of "life
against death," an unveiling of the ineffable Truth at
the heart of things. The Christian Fathers misunder-
stood the rite of mimetic marriage, it seems clear,
casting Hierophant and Priestess in roles of degradation
rather than of rites done "in silence, in darkness and
in perfect chastity" (HARRISON: 551; KERENYI: 105ff).
Clement of Alexandria, for one, declaims "the mysteries
of the atheists," "mysteries of murders and funerals,"
reciting the stories of divine acts and their liturgical
celebrations, and tracing *mystêria* to *mysos*, a defile-
ment or disgusting spectacle (*Prot.* II.13.1). Alexandria, thanks to the Ptolemies, had been given a suburban
Eleusis, where a temple of Persephone, a Koreion, included the *drama mystikon* which Clement describes (*Prot.*
II.12.2) and which he mistakes for the actual liturgy
reserved for the Attic Eleusis (KERENYI: 115ff).
Clement would also have seen the passion play of Osiris,
the chief public festival of Alexandria (ANGUS: 123ff).
The Fathers' diatribes against the mysteries reflect
the popular superstition and misinterpretation to
which the myths and rituals were subject over the years;
but behind their apologetic purpose lies a warning about
the context of need and searching which formed their
world.

Thus Mystery grew where man recognized his
plight. Caught in a wheel of rebirths, he saw the problem of fertility as symbolic of a deeper mystery, of
immortality for the creature who was more than nature
but less than divine. So out of the "things done" of
primitive religion emerged the "things acted" of mystery
cult: out of *drômena* the *drama*.

6

After centuries of epic poetry, drama sprang up in Greece, child of the Dionysian liturgy. Formally speaking, this worship involved pantomimic dances and harvest-festival "goat-songs" (*tragos*, goat). The tragic Chorus could develop only because the liturgy assumed that the worshipper may identify with the god, that the mime is effective, sacramental. Here was not only ritual singing and dancing, entrance and exit, light and darkness, pantomime and commentary; here was also the theme of all drama: birth and death, human and divine mystery, redemption the fate of man and the gods: tragedy. In time the great tragedians would develop the essential theme: "hostile transcendence," for "The fall is not the fall of man; rather, it is being that, so to speak, falls on him" (RICOEUR: 219f).

Tragedy is the imitative art of portraying the human condition in such a manner that the spectators will experience pity for the hero and terror at his fate, so being purged by the resolution of the plot. This definition of Aristotle's (*Poetics* 1449[b]. 24ff) puts its weight behind *catharsis*. Against that "background of power" called *Moira*, the tragic theme of suffering and doom is played out: "being falls on man." Yet a different reconstruction of classic drama is possible, one which envisages a larger horizon, allowing both tragedy and comedy to play their parts. The ritual contest (*agôn*) leads through death to resurrection, and thence to festive board and bed: "Agon, Sacrifice, Feast, Marriage Kômos" (MURRAY 1912: 341ff; CORNFORD 1961: 56ff; McLELLAND 1970: 80ff). Such form has ramifications, perhaps of a universal kind: "the laws of physics are the decrees of fate" (Whitehead). That is, the ritual contest of dismemberment and reconstruction, *ana-lysis*, is the theme of drama because it is the basic pattern of human thought, the rhythm of human being; and divine?

Mystery and tragedy explore a dimension integral to Greek religion, one in which there is contact with a hostile environment, anxiety before an ultimate threat. In *The Birth of Tragedy From the Spirit of Music*, Nietzsche remarked on the contrast between the

two streams of Greek experience, symbolized by Dionysos
and Apollo. The latter, god of light and order and
reason, illustrates the philosophical tradition. His
oracle at Delphi pronounced the two celebrated utterances: "Know thyself" and "Nothing too much." Now the
Delphic shrine, in time, was able to honor both these
gods (NILSSON: 41). Nietzsche also argued for a combi-
nation of the gifts and qualities they symbolized. Yet
it would seem that the Academy, especially as interpreted by modern Western philosophers, turned aside from
the poets and their message, preferring the rational
illumination of Apollo alone as sufficient to solve
life's problems.

Platonism: Optimistic Rationalism?

        It is traditional among academic philosophers
to teach the historical branch of their discipline by
starting with Thales and expounding the way in which
the Ionian "physicists" replaced the Homeric myths with
philosophical-scientific theories of "nature" (e.g.
WINDELBAND: I.23). This approach may be disputed, however, on the grounds that the idea of *physis* involved
is metaphysical for both sides, so that there is only
a formal difference between the assumptions of Homer
and Hesiod, and those of the "first philosophers."
Werner Jaeger states that "The history of Greek thought
is an organic unity, closed and complete" (JAEGER 1961:
149; cf CORNFORD 1939: 65ff; KRONER 1956: 45ff; Aristotle, *Meta.* 983^{b}f.) Cornford traces a scientific and
a mystical kind of philosophy, the one stemming from
Olympian theology, the other from the Mystery God;
Ionian and Pythagorean for example (CORNFORD 1957:
124ff). Two types of religion, two of philosophy: and
then came Plato.

        At first blush Plato seems to belong to the
demythologisers, those who displaced the Olympian theology with an optimistic rationalism. This is the way
he is taken by many, who lament the "intellectual fall
from grace" of the intuitive element in his theory of

Eidos (FRIEDLANDER: 19). On such a view, he developed
the Socratic notion that truth is inherent in the human
soul, available through a process of *anamnêsis*, and be-
longing to the realm of intelligibles; the Idea of the
Good is his answer to the problem of God. But this will
not do; not even for neophyte students of philosophy.
Plato's reliance on the power of discursive thought was
far from uncritical. He did not accept Parmenides' ontology without radical revision--here lies the heart of
the question of his influence on Western thought, on
Christian theology in particular.

Parmenides' *Way of Truth* views being as
simple, whole, immutable--predicates which Plato trans-
ferred to his archetypes (CORNFORD 1939: 34ff; cf
FRIEDLANDER: 24ff, KIRK-RAVEN: 263ff, WEIL: 74). His
famous identification of thinking and being ("it is the
same thing that can be thought and that can be"), so
fateful for Western thought, is similarly modified by
Plato. Accepting the Parmenidean distinction between
appearance and reality, he still was able to combine
"the logic of Parmenides with the other-worldliness of
Pythagoras and the Orphics" (RUSSELL: 135). This second element provided a critical stance, informed by an
intuitive or mystical note--the *daimôn* Eros, the process
of *paideia*--which allowed a freedom over naive rationalism. When Plato is viewed as an idealist philosopher
chiefly preoccupied with epistemological and political
models, we need to recall his later years at the Academy, the question of his "unwritten doctrine," of the
Letters, of what appears to have been his mature con-
cern--harmony and infinity, The Good and God, the revelation of truth (TAYLOR: 503ff).

Plato's dialogue *Parmenides* provides the key
to the development of Platonism, and to that interpre-
tive doctrine which Klibansky has called "the continuity of the Platonic tradition" (KLIBANSKY). The
dialogue's discussion of the nature of the One involves
two hypotheses, exploring the question of whether there
is a way from the One to the Many. The first hypothesis (137C-142A) accepts Parmenides' own definition

of bare or absolute unity, describable only in negations: without parts, beginning or end, shape, position, motion or rest, identity or difference, etc.
The climax of this apophatic philosophy brings us to
that later Platonism which proved so fateful for Christian theology: "There is, accordingly, no way in which
the One has being. Therefore, the One in no sense *is*
... It is not named or spoken of, not an object of
opinion or of knowledge, not perceived by any creature."

It is this One beyond all being, names and
knowledge that was to be identified with the supreme
God not only in Neoplatonism, but also in that Middle
Platonism which directly influenced the Alexandrian
Fathers. This theological interpretation may be dismissed as contrived, false to the original Plato--
Cornford remarks "What Parmenides offered to Socrates
was a gymnastic exercise, not the disclosure of a supreme divinity" (CORNFORD 1939: 131). I.M. Crombie
agrees, summarizing the argument as "There is such a
thing as unity, and it is false that it is unitary"
(CROMBIE: II.347; cf JAEGER 1947: 90ff). Yet it remains true, as Klibansky has demonstrated, that it was
this very interpretation, inflated though it may be,
which formed the crucial step in subsequent Platonism.

The second hypothesis (142B-155E) offers a
different concept of unity, according to which the One
has being and therefore shares in relationship and
knowability: "any 'One that is' is a whole and also
has parts" (142D). This complex unity, in contrast
with the simplex One, served Plotinus as model for Mind
and Soul. E.F. Osborn sees this antithesis of the One
and the One-Many combined with the antithesis of transcendent and immanent divinity as the structuring heritage for Middle and Neo-Platonism. Indeed, the critical move in this development is described by Osborn:
"While a great part of the story is the ingenious
balancing of one and many, transcendence and immanence,
the growing tendency was not to look for a *via media*
between transcendence and immanence, but to emphasize
on the one hand the transcendence of the one, and on
the other hand the immanence of the one-many" (OSBORN:
24).

Thus the philosophical tradition culminating not only in Plotinus but also and in a comparable manner in Alexandrian theology, involves at least two logical moves. First, being *qua* being was identified with God. Aristotle's thesis (*Meta*. 1073A) of Eternal Substance immovable and devoid of parts or passions, was accepted as an operational definition of God, interpreted in relation to the Platonic Parmenides, and so looking toward the theological articulation of God as Pure Being. Second, the elevation of the supreme god, as absolute One, was stressed in so extreme a manner that he is beyond intelligence. Indeed, the radical transcendence of this interpretation places deity above both intelligence and *being*--the twin emphases of Neoplatonism. The phrase "beyond being" (*Rep*. 509B, *epeikeina tês ousias*) will be echoed by Origen: God "transcends mind and being" (*C. Cels*. VII:38; cf VI:64).

Plato is more than Socrates. From his master he drew the sense of confidence in *Logos*, distrust of *Mythos*. Poets were banned, according to the *Republic* (II.377)--but by the time he wrote the *Laws* (398; cf JAEGER 1945: III.255ff), Plato had recovered his own confidence in that to which even *Logos* is but an approach. This non-Socratic element reflects the Pythagorean-Orphic tradition, the religious philosophy that takes mythology seriously. It is because of its presence, particularly in the mature Plato, that we may see the subsequent development of Platonism--through the theological speculations of Middle Platonism to the mystical theology of Neoplatonism--as not eccentric to Plato's own genius but in a real sense the answer to his philosophical quest.

Plato's use of *myth* may illustrate our contention. In the *Timaeus*, he explains his use of myth in terms of model and image. The world is itself a likeness of a rational model: any account we give of the model will share its certainty and stability, whereas an account of the likeness will be in turn merely a likeness. Proportionality is involved: "as

11

reality is to becoming, so is truth to belief ... consequently it is fitting that we should, in these matters, accept the likely story (*eikôs mythos*) and look for nothing further" (29D). Because the visible world is a changing image (*eikôn*) of an eternal model, characterized by becoming rather than being, we cannot describe it with exact or ultimate truth. The "sciences" will be hampered by this "mythical" nature of their accounts, in contrast with the rational disciplines of mathematics and dialectic. For the former is but "true belief" whereas the latter is genuine "intelligence," which "can always give a true account of itself" (51E). Physics, therefore, is *alogos*, mythical.

On the other hand are those myths to which Plato has recourse when he faces an ultimate datum that defies even the rational expression or "true account" of mathematics and dialectics. Thus after describing the myth of the soul and her habitation, he concludes, "either this or something like it is true" (*Phaedo* 115). The three great myths (*Phaedo* 110, *Gorgias* 523, *Republic* X.614) belong to this type, and have been described as representing "a gap in scientific knowledge," a "ritual myth," "a substitute for poetry and mythology ... a reform of mythology" (ZELLER: 497; JAMES 1958: 278; JOWETT: II.316ff). Paul Friedländer suggests a threefold interpretation, according to which three levels obtain: pre-dialectical at the "threshold of the Socratic world," post-dialectical leading toward the Idea, and a final stage when the myth becomes central in the work (*Phaedrus, Timaeus, Critias*) because it is "built into" its subject, the most visible presence of *Eidos*. Plato's myths, he concludes, "seem to require to be understood partly *allegorice*, partly *moraliter* or *anagogice*" (FRIEDLANDER: 171ff). Following the research of Schleiermacher and Hegel, Kierkegaard developed a significant analysis in his magisterial thesis which suggests the positive or higher purpose of the myths (KIERKEGAARD: 128ff).

Thus we may observe a twofold use of myth in Plato. When it refers to the likely or approximate accounts of mere physics, it partakes of the doubtful nature of such lower disciplines; when it refers to the higher reaches of human reasoning, it represents rather the meaningful doubt or approximation appropriate to a subject that is "beyond" full comprehension, owing to its transcendence or its eschatological dimension. This would seem to be the burden of the famous raft passage of the *Phaedo*, in which Simmias indicates the difficulty, even the impossibility, of attaining certainty about death and immortality in the present life. If one finds that the quest is impossible, let him take "the best and most irrefragable of human theories, and let this be the raft upon which he sails through life--not without risk, as I admit, if he cannot find some word of God which will more surely and safely carry him" (85).

The second use of "myth" for Plato, therefore, is not an irrational (*alogos*) one, for it is the closest approximation to the true *logos* which is possible "in the present life." We must not make too much of the phrase about "finding some word of God;" yet it is significant that it was the doctrine of the logos that carried subsequent Platonism, strongly influenced by Stoic teaching on the same subject, along the path of that religious philosophy which ultimately produced the Logos concept of Plotinus, a super-rational principle before which Plato's intelligible realm is but intermediate knowledge.

Plato's later years in the Academy apparently were characterized by a renewed concern for Pythagorean numerology. The nature of *ta mathēmatika* had developed in Neopythagorean circles to a complex doctrine in which the One is the absolute *archē*, from which springs a second, an "Indefinite Two" (see CORNFORD 1939: 3ff for Alexander Polyhistor on the Pythagorean doctrine). From these two principles issued number, and in turn, geometrical shapes: point, line, plane figures, solids, sensible bodies. The cosmic harmony--the One-Many-- expresses itself through numerical relation, although

13

"the significance of number is not exhausted by its geometrical applications" (TAYLOR: 514). We shall see that
in subsequent Platonism and historical theology, the
method of abstraction derives from this numerical mystique. This classical wedding of philosophy and mathematics was not, as it has become in contemporary Western
academia, the result of a common search for quantifiable
data; rather was it the Pythagorean insight into the
mystery of a universe which responds to musical or har-
monic structures of thought, but which continues to
maintain its harmony without yielding all its secrets
to a mathematics of mere numeration. "There is no
writing of mine about these matters, nor will there ever
be one. For this knowledge is not something that can be
put into words like other sciences; but after long-
continued intercourse between teacher and pupil, in
joint pursuit of the subject, suddenly, like light
flashing forth when a fire is kindled, it is born in
the soul and straightway nourishes itself" (*Seventh
Letter* 237C).

We are suggesting that philosophy became
"optimistic rationalism" only when viewed in isolation
from its historical place in the stream of Greek reli-
gion--or when it itself forgot that place. Its subsequent history, especially its Platonic religious philosophy, cannot be a departure, a "retrogression" and
"declension" as Harnack described Neoplatonism. Rather,
it is the logical unfolding of the genuine intention of
the great philosophers. If the answers of Platonists,
in terms of *theos* and *logos*, appear to us worse than the
answers of Plato himself (and even more so of Aristotle),
that is because we assume that whenever the two masters
suggest a transcendent reality they are bad philosophers,
and whenever they interpret transcendence as divinity
they are not philosophers at all.

By the second Christian century, Platonism
was attracted more by "Plato the hierophant" than by
Plato in any more academic dress, for it had become
"theological and otherworldly" (WITT 1937: 123. cf
DANIELOU 1955: 74ff; OSBORN: 20ff; MERLAN 1967: 14ff.
LILLA provides excellent bibliographical data in his
Introduction and 43ff). It is beyond our scope to discuss the origins of Middle Platonism (Antiochus of
Ascalon, according to Cicero) or the leading figures
such as Plutarch, Atticus, Celsus or Maximus of Tyre.
This intriguing school represents a response to an era
"hungry for religion" (KELLY: 6) and constitutes a step
toward the Neoplatonic synthesis: "it bears the mark of
a transition-stage" (COPLESTON: I.2, 196). Middle
Platonism began with certain assumptions standard for
its age, reflecting what can be termed "school-Platonism
of the second century A.D." (LILLA: 41). This scholastic basis included the highest regard for Plato and
Pythagoras along with a rejection of such views as
Epicurean atheism, the Peripatetic idea of a providence
limited to the superlunary realm, and Stoic materialism
and determination. It was eclectic, yet eager to articulate a Platonic orthodoxy.

Philip Merlan has shown that the Platonism
which culminated in Plotinus may be grasped best by
understanding Aristotle's presentation of it (MERLAN
1967: 14ff; cf 1953: 8ff). Instead of the familiar
sensible/intelligible dichotomy, a more complex relationship obtains, between a "horizontal" trichotomy
(ideas-intelligibles, mathematicals, physicals-sen-
sibles) and a "vertical" dualism. The latter is the
Two-opposite-principles doctrine, the One and the
Indefinite Dyad, functioning as universal causes,
identified with principles of good and evil, at the
last. They provide the way out of the static being of
Parmenides, allowing for plurality, for the One-Many
alternative noted already in connection with Plato's
relation to Parmenides. This complex teaching was

apparently based largely on a lecture or series
(*akroasis*) on The Good, edited by Aristotle himself.
It turned on the problem of mediating between a supreme sphere of being and the sensible world, with ideas
òr mathematicals (or ideas *as* mathematicals?) deriving
from the principles and assuming the mediatorial role.
Moreover, that *akroasis On the Good* culminated in the
statement that the good or goodness is the One.

A second source of Platonism is the teaching
of the *Letters*. Plotinus was able to adopt three dogmas in particular--of three hypostases (second Letter),
a god elevated above the artificer (sixth) and an ineffable union with the One (seventh) (ARMSTRONG 1967: 30,
93, 236ff). Whether Plato intended all this remains
doubtful; yet he had at least implied a One "beyond
knowledge and being" (*Rep.* VI.507-9), and had composed
enigmatic Letters (all accepted as authentic in anti-
quity) that offered a Plato *esotericus*; in brief,
tradition easily began where he left off. So it was
that Middle Platonism speaks clearly about a God who
transcends names and magnitudes, who may be reached by
negation and by immediate intuition. Such ideas are
found in Plutarch, in Maximus of Tyre, in Numenius--
and in Albinus. We will listen to Albinus a little,
not because he is necessarily typical (one must beware
of generalization in this area, so the Cambridge his-
torians warn us), but because his thought and even some
of his language have echoes in the Alexandrian Fathers
who are our chief concern. Besides, scholars are better
informed about him than about other Middle Platonists,
and he has been the subject of excellent research in
recent years (cf WITT; MERLAN, 1967: 64ff).

To establish his context, then, we may note
that Philip Merlan distinguishes four outstanding
varieties of Platonism by the end of the second century
A.D. 1) Aristotle and the Old Academy, continuing in
Eudorus; 2) Antiochus' syncretism of Plato, the Stoa
and probably some Aristotle; 3) the syncretism of
Albinus and Apuleius ("an almost complete synthesis of
Plato with Aristotle"); and 4) the non-syncretistic

16

system of Atticus and Plutarch. The Platonism of Celsus is chiefly polemical while Maximus of Tyre is more rhetor than philosopher (MERLAN 1967: 82f).

Albinus' *Didaskalikos* was an attempt to "discuss the principles ... of theology" (*peri tôn archôn*). There are three *archai*: matter, shapeless and without quality; ideas, the divine *paradeigmata* after which the world was fashioned; and The Good. The last is simple, incorporeal, practically incapable of formulation. He distinguishes a First God, Nous and Soul, clearly a decisive step toward Neoplatonism. The First God is unmoved, but not mover, so transcendent that he "acts" only through the Nous. Indeed, so remote is the supreme god that to call him good is false, implying ·participation in goodness. It is ineffable, without predicates, and therefore incapable of verbal expression (*arrêtos*). Albinus wavers between elevating God above intelligence --Plotinus will take the full step--and considering him a "superior Nous," an intellectual Good. He prefers the latter case, and expounds a rather scholastic *schema* which provides a clear statement of what will become in Christian theology the three "ways" of approaching deity: *via negationis, via causalitatis, via eminentiae*. For Albinus they represent three forms of one modality, the indirect knowledge which the human mind can have of One who is "not genus nor species nor difference."

The first method, which Clement will repeat almost verbatim, is described by Albinus as follows: "We shall achieve the first idea of God by making successive abstractions, just as we get the conception of a point by abstraction from what is sensible, removing first the idea of surface, then that of line, till finally we have a point" (*Epit.* X.5-6; see WITT 1937: 132f. Clement's passage is *Str.* v.XI.71). Wolfson has traced this approach to Euclid's definition of a point, reconstructed from the commentary of Simplicius: "Euclid thus defined a point negatively because it was arrived at by the subtraction of surface from body, and by the abstraction of line from surface, and by the

17

abstraction of point from line. Since then body has
three dimensions it follows that a point has none of
the dimensions, and has no part." One recognizes here
the issue of indivisible lines so important for Pythagorean and Platonic theory of mathematicals (cf CORNFORD
1939: 7ff).

Such a negative definition by means of abstraction is identical with Plotinus' method (*aphairēsis*),
and very similar to Philo's mode of predication. Yet
although Philo begins from the ineffability of God, he
does not work out a logical theory of negative attribution, but rests content with the formality of God's
causal relationship to his creation. All three, however
--Albinus, Plotinus and Philo--agree that one is able to
describe what God is *not* rather than what he is. They
also agree that other modes of apprehension function in
a complementary manner to afford a fuller description of
deity, although each philosopher has a different understanding of what the other modes are.

Albinus' critical passage continues: "A
second way of obtaining an idea of God is that of analogy, as follows: the relation which the sun has to
sight and to visible things is that, while not itself
sight, it makes it possible for the sight to see and
for visible things to be seen. The same relation exists
between the first mind and the mind of the soul and the
intelligible objects. It is not identical with the
mind of the soul but makes it possible for that mind
to conceive and for the intelligible things to be conceived, throwing light upon the truth concerning them."
The argument is borrowed from Plato who used it to
introduce his fourfold division of knowledge, rising
from things sensible to things intelligible (*Rep*. VI.
507Cff). It is argument from causality rather than
"analogy" in the strict sense of the later scholastic
via triplex. Analogy, of course, may be related to
the way of eminence or ascension as well. Albinus'
point is the familiar figure of a First Mind which
sustains the faculty of human thought, providing mental
illumination. As the ultimate cause of reasoning, this

second "way" is a kind of presupposition of the others rather than a separate mode. After the Pseudo-Dionysius (whom we shall call Denis, following Gilson) had formalized the three ways (*De div. nom.* VII.3) the scholastic tradition found it convenient to distinguish merely positive and negative attributes of God, corresponding to *viae eminentiae* and *negationis*. Hence, "the third, the *via causalitatis* was (probably rightly) interpreted by Schleiermacher and A. Schweizer as the common presupposition and crown of both, and was not actually used as a third method co-ordinated with the first two" (BARTH: II.1, 347; cf WOLFSON 1952 and 1957).

Albinus' third way corresponds to the *via eminentiae* and draws on Plato again (*Symp.* 210). "The third way of achieving an idea of God is this. One contemplates the beauty of physical objects; after this one passes on to the beauty of the soul, from there to the beauty of customs and laws, and so on to the vast ocean of the beautiful. After this one conceives the good and the lovable and the desirable like a shining light which, as it were, illumines the soul which is thus ascending. And God is comprehended together with the good because of its superior excellence." By means of these grades of ascension, the soul finds passage to the God who is linked with them in analogical proportion.

By such negative and positive moves, then, human thought and language is able to offer a true description of That which remains ineffable in its essential being. The negative attributes, we should note, are not privations by which we understand that because God is not A therefore He is B, or even that He "is" not-A. Rather they are genuine negations by which we understand that God transcends the whole polarity of A and not-A. Middle Platonism followed Aristotle's distinction of negation as against privation in this respect. Since God is beyond both virtue and wickedness, for example, he can be said to be "not good." This does not indicate a privation on his part, but the negation of his involvement within the polarity

19

described by the terms of reference. In this sense the way of negation illumines the divine transcendence, and presses forward to the development of mystical theology.

From textual bases in a few Platonic works, therefore, later Platonism developed a doctrine of God that featured a radical transcendence along with an emerging trinity which Plotinus would describe as The One, Spirit and Soul. It is clear that "the elevation of the supreme god over intelligence and the attendant doctrine that he is accessible only through some supra-rational act has become rather generally accepted by the time of Plotinus" (MERLAN 1967: 80n; LILLA: 212ff). Plotinus was able and free to develop the loaded inter-pretation of Plato, particularly of his *Parmenides,* where the first hypothesis about The One (142A) was taken as implying a God beyond all being, unknowable, subject to merely negative attribution (cf HENRY: XXXIX). It is this interpretation, present in the centuries leading to Neoplatonism, that necessitates some modifi-cation of Wolfson's thesis, which may be summed up in two sentences: "This distinction between the knowabi-lity of God's existence and the unknowability of his essence was something new in Greek philosophy. It was introduced by Philo ... once these terms (ineffable, unnamable, incomprehensible) were used by Philo they begin to occur frequently in Greek philosophy" (WOLFSON 1965: 6; cf 1947: II.111ff). S. Lilla, however, points out that both E.R. Dodds and A.J. Festugière have drawn attention to the history of the Platonic doctrine; he concludes, "It is therefore very likely that Philo, though having in mind the scriptural passages to which Wolfson has drawn attention, took into account also the speculations on the 'one' of the Parmenides which were current in the Neopythagorean schools of his time" (LILLA: 218).

Sooner or later one comes to Alexandria, where Philo occupies his unique position in the story of both Platonism and its Christian form; and where Plotinus later sat under Ammonius Saccas. Plotinus will bring the development we have been sketching to its climax in the familiar passage *Enneads* VI, 7, 36: "Knowing of the Good or contact with it, is the all-important: this--we read--is the grand learning, the learning, we are to understand, not of looking towards it but attaining, first, some knowledge of it. We come to this learning by analogies, by abstractions, by our understanding of its subsequents, of all that is derived from The Good, by the upward steps towards it ... we are near now, the next is That and it is close at hand, radiant above the Intellectual. Here, we put aside all the learning; disciplined to this pitch, established in beauty, the quester holds knowledge still of the ground he rests on, but, suddenly, swept beyond it all by the very crest of the wave of Intellect surging beneath, he is lifted and sees, never knowing how."

We shall pick up certain threads of this Platonic story in our final chapter. Meanwhile, the one who must come before us next is Philo, since his work is of direct consequence for the Christian Fathers of Alexandria. Their kind of Platonism is not explicable in terms of historical philosophy alone. They lived and taught in a City that occupied a unique position in ancient culture; and Philo represents that position in a significant way.

CHAPTER 2

PHILO : THE MODEL

The City

      Founded by Alexander the Great in 332/331 B.C., the city of Alexandria was neither Egyptian nor Greek, but "the birthplace of Hellenism" (QUASTEN: II.1), "carrefour de toutes les sagesses de l'Orient" (CROUZEL 1962: 169). This commingling of Oriental, Egyptian and Greek cultures gave rise to a new civilization. A brilliant intellectual life flourished, centered in the great royal (Ptolemy Soter) foundations of Library and Museum. The one contained an estimated 500,000 volumes; the other was a sort of University, where public lecture halls echoed to the continuing discussion of comparative philosophy. The twin phenomena associated with Alexandrian thought were scepticism and eclecticism (DRUMMOND: I.6f). By the second century A.D. it could be described as cosmopolitan, syncretistic, creative; "a sort of clearing house for the religions of the Roman Empire" (GILSON: 29).

      Egypt as a whole and Alexandria in particular are significant for the origin and growth of the Wisdom literature, of Gnosticism and of the Hermetic writings. The earliest example of wisdom in this historical sense seems to be "The Teaching of Amen-em-ope" from the eighth century B.C. The Jewish apocryphal "Wisdom of Solomon" was composed in the city in the first century B.C. There had been, in the Sibylline Oracles, an instance of Jewish apologetics cast in Greek form; but The Wisdom of Solomon was a Jewish form conveying Hellenistic substance. God is Being, Wisdom a genuine hypostasis, having attributes far beyond the usage of *Proverbs* 8. Wisdom is only-begotten, present through all things, the divine agent in creation and renewal. In contrast, the concept of Logos remains inchoate, not yet identified with Wisdom or elevated to the status to which Philo will assign it.

The rise of Gnosticism remains a complex problem, as to whether it is a wholly Christian phenomenon
(cf HARNACK 1961: I.227ff, II.169ff; JONAS; R.M. GRANT
1961; WILSON). Whatever one's judgment on this question,
the two greatest Gnostics are associated with Egypt.
Basilides laboured there, while Valentinus was said by
Epiphanius to have been "educated after the Greek
fashion in Alexandria." We shall have occasion to reflect on this problem when we consider the Alexandrian
Fathers. For in Gnostic teaching there is a cluster of
concepts which press the Platonic tradition already
noted to its theological conclusion: an absolute, unknown God, apprehended only by the only-begotten Mind;
the supreme God is now lost in Abyss, best described as
non-existent. The Hermetic corpus grew out of the distinctively Egyptian gnosis (FESTUGIERE: IV).

What of the original Christian Church in
Egypt? Harnack has underlined the conclusion of Over-
beck, about "the well-defined dark region on the map
of the ecclesiastical historian of this period," namely
Alexandria. Until the episcopate of Demetrius, 180 A.D.,
we know nothing of events. At that point there emerges
"a stately church with that school of higher learning
attached to it by means of which its influence was to
be diffused and its fame borne far and wide" (HARNACK
1961: II.323). We do know much more about the Jewish
community in the city, where the figure of Philo marks
a culmination and a watershed. We know also of the
lectures of Ammonius Saccas, attended by another crucial figure, Plotinus. And we know--by now it is the
second century A.D.--of the catechetical "school of
higher learning" of Clement and Origen.

This was the City. As the Christian era
progressed it would see great battles fought, first
around the name of its greatest son, Origen, and then
around its later children Arius and Athanasius. It
was to be the leading theological center of the early
church. In time the Muslim faith would arrive,
leaving its Christian episode behind, and its heritage
of ambiguity scattered East and West in Christendom.

24

It was in the Jewish community of Alexandria that the ideas of East and West were "first blended in fruitful union" (BIGG: 2). The Jews were, according to Philo, a million strong in Egypt, and particularly rich and powerful in Alexandria. Their production of the Septuagint about 150 B.C. illustrates the hellenistic cast of thought. In this Greek translation of the Hebrew scripture, written especially for the Diaspora, a subtle but significant choice of language suggests the shift in understanding of God. This problem sits on slippery ground, since it seems to assume the sharp dichotomy between Hebrew and Greek language and thought which remains the subject of sharp debate. It may be that T.F. Torrance presses the point too hard in stating, "the thought of the Hebrew O.T. is greatly impoverished in the LXX, and particularly at the very point where the O.T. bears the full seed of the N.T. *charis*" (TORRANCE 1948: 19). Yet in key passages on the divine action and the divine name (e.g. *Gen.* 6:6, *Lev.* 24:15ff, *Deut.* 32:8) there is evidence of the influence of that idea of ontological transcendence and its concomitant immutability and impassibility of which we are speaking (DRUMMOND: 157; DAVIES: 11f; cf GUTTMANN: 18ff). Moreover, as our concluding sections will claim, the contemporary debate on dehellenization involves a more profound analysis of the role of language than the philosophy of "linguistic analysis" provides (cf DEWART 1969: 120ff).

Such shift in the concept of God involves the avoidance of anthropomorphic phrases wherever possible, but is particularly significant in the handling of the divine *name*. The Hebrew tetragrammaton YHVH is translated chiefly by the Greek *Kyrios*, "Lord." Philo will interpret *Kyrios* and *Theos* as representing two distinct divine attributes, love and justice. This interpretation was strengthened by the LXX usage of translating the Hebrew *hesed* by *dikaiosynē* and *eleos*, thus introducing an unhebraic tension.

25

Exodus chapter 3 is the classic passage regarding the divine name. The cryptic Hebrew of verse 14 is best translated by some statement of personal affirmation: "I am ..." followed by first-person attributes. But the LXX has *egō eimi ho ōn*. God is now "He Who Is," a third person Being. It is a modality less dynamic than the Hebrew, although still more than the static *To On* of the Eleatic definition. It is, indeed, reflective of the school-Platonism already noted, of the general preoccupation with transcendence and its corollary, the hypostatization of mediators. The Rabbinic tradition had also speculated about the mediatorial function of the High Priest, about the wisdom (*Memrah*) or creative word of God, and about the four living creatures of Ezekiel's vision, whom they unified as "The Charioteer."

Such was the spirit of the age, and the literary context, of the city and community which Philo inherited. He was to incarnate this spirit in a remarkable manner, and to produce a theology based on the Septuagint as interpreted through hellenistic ideas. Such a hellenized biblical theology reflects the crucial turn which Philo gave to the Platonic dualism and in turn to Christian theism: "The original gnosis is the theology of Jewish Christianity" (DANIELOU 1964: 54).

Philo and Logos

A contemporary of St. Paul, Philo Judaeus of Alexandria was heritor of rabbinic speculation, hellenistic philosophy and Egyptian wisdom. Yet he is more than merely eclectic, for he brings an original touch which makes him a crucial figure, whom one modern philosopher is promoting as the foundational thinker (until Spinoza) for the religious philosophy of Judaism, Christianity and Islam (WOLFSON 1947).

"As early as Philo, we see that the current intellectual coin of the more literate classes of society is this blend of Stoic ethics with Platonic

26

metaphysics and some Aristotelian logic. Like the form
of Greek spoken in the hellenistic world, it is a philosophical *koinê*, and Philo simply takes it for granted"
(CHADWICK 1966: 6). We have seen that this *koinê* involved ideas of a supreme being of extreme transcendence
coupled with an emerging importance assigned to intermediaries such as Nous, Sophia and Logos. We also noted
the significance of the Alexandrian Jewish text *The Wisdom of Solomon*. This talked of Logos as well as Wisdom,
sharing divine attributes and essence. Finally, the
Heraclitean doctrine was popular in Alexandria, providing a sort of motto: "The wise is one thing, to be
acquainted with true judgment, how all things are
steered through all" (*Frag.* 41--KIRK-RAVEN: 204).

Heraclitus' logos, although the source of
rationality in the cosmos, was not itself a conscious
intelligence. Plato, like Anaxagoras, chose Nous as
his principle of rationality; it was rather the Stoic
teaching which invested Logos with the functions of an
active principle, particularly through the distinctive
form as *logos spermatikos* (BREHIER: 83ff). For Heraclitus, "riddler" and "obscure," Logos suggested the
kind of dialectic which obtains to achieve that
"balanced strife between opposites" of his theory of
flux. It signifies a proportionality, which the human
mind grasps as it recognizes "how all things are
steered through all" (cf WHEELWRIGHT: 107).

The term *logos* is described by Gilbert Murray
as "the most characteristic word in the Greek language,"
lying at the root of philosophy, science and religion
(MURRAY 1953: 27). Its destiny was to offer a comprehensive term under which could be subsumed a variety of
similar concepts--the Platonic forms, the Heraclitean
formula, the Stoic pantheism. The Stoics shaped it
most precisely, taking the Heraclitean fire-flux
seriously, and making it applicable through the *logoi
spermatikoi*. What had been a growing tendency to relate the twin poles of God and Matter through some intermediary was given clearer expression and greater
importance in the emerging notion of Logos. Arguing

27

against the Platonic idealism, the Stoics took some
hints from the Peripatetic natural philosophy and phy-
siology, and developed a materialistic conception.
Philo holds the key to this emerging notion. He sketched
a figure having its own life-principle within itself in
the form of logos. The cosmic Logos is present in every
object and person as seminal logos. The Stoic imagery of
seed, sowing, the continual renewal of life, allows the
monistic cosmos to yet pulse with a rhythm of *logos endiathetos* and *logos prophorikos*. The inward and the expressed word are linked with another way of putting their
case, the doctrine of Nature as *Pneuma*. Heraclitus' fire
continues to warm and to stir the universe, now as the
vital breath or Pneuma. And because of the inevitable
principle of correspondence between universe and man--
macrocosmos and microcosmos--there is a psychology and
an ethics, a pneumatic reflection of cosmic unity and a
morality of harmony with nature (CAIRD: II.103ff).

This familiar set of concepts influenced Philo
and the Christian Fathers in numerous ways (SPANNEUT;
CAIRD: II.347ff). Not least is the Stoic anthropology:
it is rational to live in harmony with nature, i.e. conformity with reason. This circular argument appealed to
generations struggling with the problem of evil and the
role of the passions. As man matures (attains rationality) he is afflicted with the opposite of reason,
passion: pleasure and pain, desire and fear. Passion
is not natural, but is "an irrational movement of the
soul contrary to nature, or an impulse in excess" (ZENO,
in DRUMMOND: II.115). The passions belong to the lesser
epistemological realm of *doxa*, mere opinion, although
they serve to mark the stages of growth, the testing of
one's judgment (*krisis*). When man matures, he lives by
reason alone, so that a passionless calm characterizes
him. This control of *pathê* through harmony with divinity will recur as a theme in Christian theology down
the centuries.

The problem of interpreting the history of the
logos concept is most difficult. There are those who
claim that too much has been read back into the fragments

from Heraclitus; that the Stoic theory of *logoi sperma-tikoi* is merely biological; and that Philo's attribution of *Memrah* qualities to Logos was a religious move and not a philosophical one (HODGSON 217f; DODD 263ff). The interpretation of Heraclitus remains problematic; thus, "The English word that best covers Heraclitus' philosophical uses of 'Logos' is 'formula'" (EP: III.477[b]). Richard Kroner will not admit "any trace of ontology" in Heraclitus, and disputes Heidegger's reading of *logos* from *legein* (KRONER 1956: 100). The Platonic Ideas were assimilated to the *logoi*: "Philo is the earliest witness to the doctrine that the Ideas are God's thoughts" (CHADWICK 1967: 142). That is, Philo distinguished the logoi or intelligibles from Logos itself, and made it explicit that the former are ideas in the divine mind (*Opif*. 18, 55; *Cher*. 49). This was to become of great significance for medieval thought, as the problem of universals (WOLFSON 1947: I.294). Philo identifies the Ideas with the Powers; these *dynameis* function much like the *energeia* of later Byzantine theology.

The Logos is God's Reason, the Idea of ideas (*Migr*. 103), the "archetype and model," "a pre-existent abstract idea" for the creation of intelligence or "archetypal wisdom" (*Leg. All*. I.22, 43 cf *Opif*. 25). "God is the most generic thing, and the Logos of God is second" (*Leg. All*. II.86). The Logos has God for its father and Wisdom for mother (*Fug*. 20, 109), although sometimes Logos and Sophia are identified (cf WOLFSON 1947: I.253ff). Logos is closest to God, the eternal reason which regulates the cosmos, akin to Heraclitus' unity of opposites (*Quis Rer*. 43). He recognizes a duality in man, yet refrains from applying the dialectic of *endiathetos* and *prophorikos* to the Logos itself (*V. Mos*. 3.13). Although all knowledge is the result of rational illumination, we must not stick even at Logos but persist to the divinity beyond (*Leg. All*. III.31f).

Philo's Logos looms large as a transitional step toward the fulness of trinitarian speculation. Chadwick warns us that it is "no more than a stage,"

in the sense that Philo does not attend to those passages in Plato (*Parmenides* and *Letters*) that were to
prove crucial "in giving authority to the Neoplatonic
Triad" (CHADWICK 1967: 145). Nevertheless, Philo's
relating of Logos to intelligibles proved a decisive
step, until by the elevation of Logos above the ideal
realm, the Christian Fathers used it as a concept far
beyond Philo's intention.

Allegory

Philo's second chief contribution, beside the
doctrine of the Logos, was the allegorical method of
biblical exegesis. The historical beginnings of allegory have been described by modern scholars and need
not be detailed here (e.g. ZELLER: III.i, 322; R.M.
GRANT 1957; HANSON 1959. For Philo cf WOLFSON 1947:
I.115ff and DRUMMOND: I.121ff). It is worth noting,
however, that Philo inherits both philosophical and
theological traditions of allegory. The exegetes of
Homer, notably the Stoics, followed Plato's demytholo-
gizing method and interpreted the anthropomorphisms of
Homer and Hesiod allegorically. Assuming the poetic
"inspiration" of their texts, they could approach them
"scientifically" (*physikōs*), thus accommodating the
myths to their philosophy. Since *names* provide a key
to meaning—they believed that names participate in
the power of what is named—they could argue for a
deeper or non-literal meaning through understanding
names.

Jewish exegetes followed suit. Aristobulus
interpreted the O.T. anthropomorphisms *physikōs*, as did
the community of Therapeutae near Alexandria, whom
Philo commends for their method (they "seek wisdom
from their ancestral philosophy by taking it as an
allegory"—*V. contempl.* 3). Philo dislikes both Jewish
traditionalists who reject philosophy and allegorical
exegesis, and certain "extreme allegorists" who retire
from the world to serve God as "individual recluses"

30

(WOLFSON 1947: I.66ff). In general, Jewish exegesis
had not developed any systematic typology, in part
because of its lack of interest in eschatology and
Messianic speculation. "Alexandrian Jewish scholars
neither inherited nor themselves formed a range of
technical terms in which to express their allegory.
That was a task left for Alexandrian Christian scholars
to accomplish" (HANSON 1959: 41).

The question which is at issue here and in
the Christian Fathers concerns the relationship between
philosophy and biblical exegesis. It may be examined
in light of the concept of *mystery*. For Philo, mystery
religion provides a thematic way to expound the allegorical interpretation of texts. So insistent is the
language of the mysteries indeed that modern scholars
from Conybeare to Goodenough have maintained that Philo
transformed Judaism into a Mystery, with the Mosaic
Law as *hieros logos,* and God as the Absolute related
to the world by "His Light-Stream, the Logos or Sophia"
(GOODENOUGH 1935: 7; cf WOLFSON 1947: I.44f; CHADWICK
1967: 152).

Philo does indeed distinguish lesser and
greater mysteries, as Clement will in turn, casting
the religious life as a passage from the passions
through reason to "a clear vision" of God (*Sacr.* 16,
62; *Leg. All.* III.100; *Migr.* 27ff). But it is philosophy which functions as the "synthetic *a priori*" for
Philo's epistemology: as he takes knowledge of God
and man through the scriptures, he develops categories
already implied by the abstract and ideational nature
of his philosophical commitment. Therefore he adopts
the language of the mysteries as a way to collate
philosophy with scripture, an apologetic for his
handling of the sacred text. If religion is a mystery,
a *transitus* from passion to reason, from emotional decision to rational contemplation, then one must approach every text with a suspicion, an expectation
that before one stands "the nature which loves to hide
itself" (*Fug.* 32, 179). This same passage refers to
those "not initiated (*amuêtoi*) in allegory." For

Philo, the covenant with Israel is God's gift of "the true ... the infallible mysteries of the Existent" (*Immut.* 62). Allegory as a method derives from the ontological premise that God is beyond every sensible occasion of knowledge, and the anthropological corollary that man is called to ascend beyond every literal, historical and sensible text and event.

The Divine Name

Philo's definition of God as The Existent (*to on*) is more like a formula than a confession of faith. It appears to be somewhat beyond the LXX *ho ōn*, in the direction of an abstract pure Being. God is the One or Monad, beyond multiplicity (*Leg. All.* III.48; *Immut.* 11f). So transcendent is he, indeed, that he is said to be even "beyond the Monad" (*Leg. All.* II.3; *Praem.* 40). The classic theological question of predication or attribution is before us in a precious form. For Philo is caught between his religious instinct and his philosophical *a priori*. The question concerns both Philo himself and the Alexandrian theology to follow: is there an irreconcilable contradiction between the negative and the positive attributes of God? That is, is the negative mode so emphasized that it is the controlling one, the ultimate predication?

The symbolism of *names* helps Philo to some extent. Names are "characters of powers" or "marks of capacities" (*Mut.* 65). Thus the two chief names for God in scripture, *theos* and *kyrios*, denote the two elements to which all attribution points, namely justice and love. Both are combined (unequally, since the grace or kindness of God is the stronger) in the Logos. "The appellations which have been mentioned indicate the powers around the self-existing Being, for that of 'Lord' denotes the power according to which he rules, and that of 'God' the one according to which he benefits" (*Plant.* 20; cf *Abr.* 24f). Thus the "powers" function as divine predicates, even

32

though in a higher sense God is without qualities (*apoios*).

The extremism of the doctrine of transcendence shared by the "philosophical *koinê*" of Philo's age pressed the problem of mediation most insistently. The Existent cannot come into contact with the world of created reality. An indirect relationship is possible through the Powers which originate in the Logos, divine image and idea. He is "brought within ken by the powers that follow and attend Him; for these make evident not His essence (*ousia*) but His subsistence (*hyparxis*) from the things which He accomplishes" (*Post. C.* 169).

The Existent is both invisible and incomprehensible (*akatalēptos*) so that whatever is spoken about him as if he were visible or comprehensible to man is by way of metaphor or allegory, in accommodation to human weakness or to the baser sort of believer. "It is a logical consequence that no personal name even can be properly assigned to the truly Existent. Note that when the prophet desires to know what he must answer to those who ask about His name He says 'I am He that IS' (*Ex.* iii.14), which is equivalent to 'My nature is to be, not to be spoken' ... So impossible to name indeed is the Existent that not even the Powers who serve Him tell us a proper name" (*Mut.* 11, 14). God has no proper name, being referred to as He Who Is. Time after time Philo comments on Exodus 3:14. "At first say unto them, I am that I am, that when they have learnt that there is a difference between him that is and him that is not, they may be further taught that there is no name whatever that can properly be assigned to me, who am the only being to whom existence belongs" (*V. Mos.* I.14; cf *Somn.* I.39f). But to this existential denotation is added a historical one--the names of Abraham, Isaac and Jacob are involved: "having added his own pecular name to their names he has united them together, appropriating to himself an appellation compassed of the three names" (*Abr.* 10). Though God lacks a proper name, there is the "many-titled name of God" (*Dec. Orac.* 19). A list of such titles fills a page (DRUMMOND: II.63). Again, the tetragrammaton occupies a special place; for instance, on the High Priest's headdress, "by which letters they say that the name of the living God is indicated" (*V. Mos.* III.14). Only one name, therefore, stands nearest God (*ho ōn* - *Abr.* 24). His "proper name" is the tetragrammaton (*kyrion onoma* - *Mut.* 2, 11, etc; *Somn.* 1; cf WOLFSON 1947: I.121; DANIELOU 1964: 147ff).

For Philo it is axiomatic that knowing and naming are correlative activities of the human mind. The key passage of the *De Mutatione Nominum* (7-11) illustrates the progress from the problem of genuine human knowledge of the Existent to that of a trustworthy divine name. His analysis of Ex. 3:14 concludes that the tetragrammaton means "My nature is to be, not to be spoken." Then he states, "Yet that the human race should not totally lack a title to give to the supreme goodness He allows them to use by licence of language, as though it were His proper name, the title of Lord God of the three natural orders, teaching, perfection, practice, which are symbolized in the records of Abraham, Isaac and Jacob ... Those who are born into mortality must needs have some substitute for the divine name, so that they may approach if not the fact at least the name of the supreme excellence and be brought into relation with it."

The patriarchs--taken allegorically, of course--represent not so much any historicizing of the divine being, as a progress in mystical awareness. Moses suggests the highest stage, since his experiences on the holy mountain before and after the Exodus recount his nearness to God. Ex. 20:21 says, "Moses drew near to the thick cloud where God was"--by this is indicated that he entered "into the unseen and invisible and incorporeal essence" (*V. Mos.* I.28; cf *Mut.* 2). Moses' search was not altogether fruitless, since to realize that Being is incomprehensible is

34

itself a great boon (*Post. C.* 14) The Existent is "not relative" but "full of Himself and sufficient for Himself," therefore He may be spoken of only "by licence of language" (*Mut.* 27). The higher student or "comrade of the soul" perseveres beyond the comparison of God to created entities. "They have dissociated Him from every category or quality, for it is one of the facts which go to make His blessedness and supreme felicity that His being is apprehended as simple being, without other definite characteristics; and thus they do not picture it with form, but admit to their minds the conception of existence only" (*Immut.* 55).

To be without quality (*apoios*) is to remain unknowable in essence. Man can know *that* God exists; *what* he is remains incomprehensible. It is clear that Philo makes this explicit, and that it will become foundational for Christian theology. Wolfson claims that it is equally clear that Philo originated this distinction, going beyond preceding philosophers to declare the essential incomprehensibility of God, and the consequent impossibility of naming him. We looked at this thesis in the first chapter, where we saw that speculation on the One among Platonists antedates Philo's doctrine, so that Wolfson's claim lacks the clear evidence he presumes. Yet he is right to say that neither Plato nor Aristotle states explicitly that God is incomprehensible in essence, and that Philo's statements are inescapable. "God is unnameable and ineffable and in every way incomprehensible" (*Somn.* I.67; cf. *Immut.* 13, 62; *Post. C.* 166ff). Plato's famous declaration of *Timaeus* 28C is part of the story: "The maker and father of this universe it is difficult to discover; nor, if he were discovered, could he be declared to all men." Was Plato stressing the inherent difficulty of knowing God, or did he intend the different question of communicating theological data? Is the problem ontological or noetic? Philosophers had considered it the latter, there being no *essential* unknowability about the divine. But in the Platonic speculations culminating in Middle and Neo-Platonism there is genuine suggestion of essential

35

unknowability. This is the basis on which Festugière, for example, refutes Norden's thesis (in *Agnostos Theos*) that since Greek thought could *not* have said that God is unknowable, we must conclude Oriental influence (FESTUGIERE: IV.1ff). By the time of Proclus, for instance, there might well be such influence, but there is sufficient evidence from an earlier period--Albinus in particular--reflecting the Platonic and Pythagorean traditions, to sustain Festugière's argument. He does make the important point, however, that the term *agnôstos* is ambiguous, meaning either unknown (and so patient of modalities of knowledge) or unknowable. Albinus can say, as noted above, that God is *arrêtos*, and can then develop ways of attaining knowledge of him. It would seem, therefore, that Wolfson's thesis, though stated too categorically, nevertheless indicates the unique position which Philo enjoys in this topic (WOLFSON 1947: II.113ff).

The debate among Wolfson, Norden and Festugière need not detract from the evident clarity which Philo brings to the articulation of the unknowability of God. "When therefore the God-loving soul probes the question of the essence of the Existent Being, he enters on a quest of that which is beyond matter and beyond sight. And out of this quest there accrues to him a vast boon, namely to apprehend that the God of real Being is apprehensible by no one, and to see precisely this, that He is incapable of being seen" (*Post. C.* 15). To be without qualities is to exist *sui generis*. In Philo's philosophy, God exists in a unique way because he is above qualities; matter because it is below. These are the two poles of the Platonic universe: the self-existent One tending to exist beyond existence, the other tending toward non-being. Quality is a shared attribute and therefore inapplicable to God; but one may attribute certain *properties* that are incommunicable --e.g. aseity, omnipotence, perfection. Philo thus limits the (Aristotelian) predicables attributable to God to that of property, excluding genus, accident and definition. One might argue that Philo's intention throughout his philosophical theology is to substantiate the unique divine property of *acting*. "It is the property of God to act (*to poiein*), which property we do not ascribe to any created being, for the property of the created is to suffer action (*to paschein*)" (*Cher.* 77). But his abstract methodology, involving remotion or abstraction, constantly betrays that intention.

This problem, familiar to Philonic scholars, is not easily resolved. His concept of God ascribes such properties as eternity and causality to the divine as primary (e.g. *Leg. All.* II.1), since God is self-determining Mind, Cause of all. Causality, of course, involves an archetypal function--that complex unity already noted in the *Parmenides*, according to which God is no bare unity but a manifold of truth, goodness and beauty in which men may participate (*Leg. All.* II.21). God is the fountain of intelligibles (*Mut.* 1), the Sun of the sun (*Sacr.* 4), "an archetypal essence of which myriads of rays are the effluence, none visible to sense, all to the mind" (*Cher.* 28). God does not participate in the rational but rules it, "being the fountain of the most ancient Logos ... archetype of rational nature" (*Det.* 22f). In this context we should note that the human mind is also and similarly incomprehensible, we do not know its essence: "Those who do not know the *ousia* of their own soul, how shall they give an accurate account of the soul of the universe?" (*Leg. All.* I.30; cf *Mut.* 2, *Cher.* 20, 32).

Rationality involves a superiority over the changing nature of creation, realm of becoming. Before turning to the question of the sort of human life commensurate with the contemplation of being, we should note further this concept of immutability.

Immutability and Impassibility

"How should one come to believe God? By learning that all other things change but He is unchangeable (*atreptos*)" (*Leg. All.* II.89). Philo's

37

handling of the concept of immutability is ethical rather than ontological. When he says that "unchangeableness is the property of God" (*Leg. All.* II.33) he intends to illustrate God's faithfulness and trustworthiness. The divine immutability is shown best when contrasted with human mutability. Abraham, for instance, "knew that God stands with place unchanged, yet moves the universal frame of creation, His own motion being the motion of self-extension ... whereby He shows His unalterable, unchanging nature. (Abraham) knew that he himself is never set in a stable position, that he is ever subject to various changes, and that throughout his life, which is one long slipping, he trips and falls, woe to him! and how great is that fall" (*Mut.* 54f). Of the Existent, therefore, Abraham could say, "it is He alone Who stands" and "all below Him are subject to change and mutation of every kind." "He Himself stands ever steadfast, while His creation wavers and inclines in opposite directions" (*Leg. All.* II.83).

Such knowledge of God and his works creates despair, but learning of the nothingness of all things leads to knowledge of the Existent (*Migr.* 33). In another place (*Somn.* I.158) Philo uses Platonic imagery to make his point: God is like "a charioteer high over his chariot or a helmsman high over his ship." He has made the universe to depend on him, for "the sure God is the support and stay, the firmness and stability of all things, imparting as with the impress of a seal to whom He will the power of remaining unshaken (*asaleuton*)." The doctrine of providence is strong in Philo: God is leader and king (*Conf.* 33), "the Archon of the great city" (*Dec. Orac.* 12).

Both space and time are relevant to Philo's discussion. The term "place" (*topos*) means either physical space, or the divine word "which God Himself has completely filled throughout with incorporeal potencies" (*Somn.* I.62), or thirdly God himself as he who contains everything without being contained--"He is Himself the space which holds Him" (*Somn.* I.63).

Similarly, temporal description cannot be applied to God: "He has made the boundaries of the ages subject to Himself. For God's life is not a time, but eternity, which is the archetype and pattern of time" (*Immut.* 32). The divine perfection involves power over spatial and temporal existence, so that in turn it redounds to his creatures. For it is his *will* that is immutable, holding fast to his purpose, "the Imperishable Blessed One" (*Immut.* 26).

Immutability and impassibility are correlative ideas, related to the anthropomorphism and anthropopathism of religious texts. Philo is guided by two Mosaic maxims: "God is as a man" (*Deut.* 1:31) and "God is not as a man" (*Num.* 23:19). Statements according to the former are accommodations to human weakness, "introduced for the instruction of the many ... for training and admonition, not because God's nature is such." When taken literally, they are nothing more than "the mythical fictions of the impious, who, professing to represent the deity as of human form, in reality represent Him as having human passions." When a passion is attributed to God, it is so metaphorically (*tropikē*), "to bring out a vital truth." The foregoing argument, from *Immut.* 52-71, could be repeated easily (e.g. *Sacr.* 28ff, *Migr.* 20, *Conf.* 27) for it is the heart of his allegorical method. The distinction in sense or meanings corresponds to a distinction between two sorts of people: bodily and spiritual; "some men are friends of the soul, others of the body" (*Immut.* 55). To recognize metaphor or allegory is a sign of progression, for the "higher student" is an initiate into the true mysteries of the Existent. For God, as "divine Legislator," uses such images to draw the initiate away from the body and its passions. God "distinctly appears to him who escapes from material things and mounts up into the incorporeal (*asōmaton*) soul of this body of ours" (*Det.* 159). The "body lovers" stick at the maxim "God is as a man" and approach him in fear; they are so impressed with the image "that they suppose that this image is not a copy,

but that what they see is the original itself." (*Somn.*
I.232).

The initiate or gnostic progresses to the
other maxim, "God is not as a man," knowing that "God
will not admit of similitude or comparison or analogy"
(*Qu. Gen.* 11.54). The entire work *Quod Deus Immuta-*
bilis Sit is an obvious reference. The "comrades of
the soul" at last "hold converse with intelligible incorporeal natures," not comparing the Existent to anything created, but admitting "the conception of existence only" in dissociation from "every category or
quality" (55). The key to such spiritual knowledge is,
not to "overlay the conception of God with any of the
attributes of created being:" "He is not apprehensible
even by the mind, save in the fact that He is. For it
is His existence that we apprehend, and of what lies
outside that existence nothing" (62). Instead of fear
there is now love--"to love Him is the most suitable
for those unto whose conception of the Existent no
thought of human parts or passions enters, who pay Him
the honor meet for God for His own sake only" (69).
We are now engaged with Philo's mystical theology, a
construction of the soul's journey and its goal that
will become part of the historical theology of the
Church both East and West.

The Vision of Ecstasy

The dynamic of Philo's thought is the soul's
union with God. "For in very deed only the unchanging
soul can draw near to the unchanging God, and the soul
in such a condition veritably stands beside the divine
power" (*Post. C.*27). Such correspondence, in the Platonic world before us, inevitably leads to the dictum
"to become like God, as far as this is possible"
(*Theaet.* 176B). Philo echoes this motto, for "the
goal of happiness is to become like God" (*Decal.* 73;
cf *Fug.* 63 - WOLFSON 1947: II.194ff). The body is a
medium for the lower life, an occasion for self-love.
It is not essentially evil, but its transiency and

mutability contrast with the eternal ideas and the life of reason. Here is Philo's dilemma: as a Platonist he can use the strongest language to score the body's perverse influence, a plotter against the soul preventing communion with God (*Leg. All.* III.13f, 22) and a prison from which the mind must flee, as Moses left the camp (*Quis Rer.* 14) or Abraham departed from Haran (*Migr.* 32ff). Yet he can also accept it as God's good creation, an inferior being necessary for the manifestation of the superior (*Leg. All.* III.23).

The geographic imagery of leaving Haran or Egypt or the camp recurs often enough to underline Philo's mystical path. One must go beyond attachment to the body, as the Fathers departed their earthly places (*Migr.* 27, *Det.* 159). Prepared by ascetic exercises, knowledge of God is a flight into pure Being, achieved in the fervent silence of mystic vision. Philo takes *ekstasis* literally: "escape from thyself also, and go forth from (*ekstêthi*) thyself, filled with a divine frenzy like those possessed in the mystic rites of the Corybantes, and held by the Deity after the manner of prophetic inspiration" (*Quis Rer.* 69; cf *Opif.* I.19). There seems a displacement of reason by exalted spirit in this experience: "the spirit, apart from the body, begins to be inwardly so inspired and initiated in divine things as to be possessed almost wholly by God" (*Qu. Gen.* IV.140). Again, "the reason within us leaves its abode at the arrival of the divine Spirit, but when the Spirit departs the reason returns to its place" (*Quis Rer.* 249). In other contexts, however, Philo can describe the ecstatic reason as separated only from the *uttered* word: "Ecstasy, as the word itself evidently points out, is nothing else than a departure of the mind (*nous*) wandering beyond itself" (*Qu. Gen.* III.9). Philo's doctrine involves a fourfold distinction among the orders of inspiration (*Quis Rer.* 51f) not unrelated to the ascent from lesser to greater mysteries (*Cher.* 49; *Sacr.* 62; *Abr.* 122). The highest level is achieved when the divine spirit rests on the prophet, creating a state equivalent to ecstasy (WOLFSON 1947: II.24ff).

The mystic silence is beyond speech; but whether the inward reason or logos remains is ambiguous in Philo. It would seem that it does, since inspired prophecy is not divorced from "interpretation." That is, even though he says that "interpretation (*hermêneia*) and prophecy (*prophêteia*) are not the same thing" (*Mos.* II.191), he makes it clear to his Greek readers that the scriptural teaching is that "prophets are interpreters of God" (*Spec.* I.65 in WOLFSON 1947: II.42). Philo's contribution to mystical theology is to insist on an element of divine inspiration or grace, and to reckon such inspiration as a form of knowledge of God. The highest knowledge is a kind of vision; higher than Ishmael the hearer is Israel, meaning "seeing God" (*Post. C.* 63; *Immut.* 144). The "comrades" may see (*idein*) the Existent, or his Logos, "For to philosophize is nothing else but to desire to see things exactly as they are" (*Conf.* 97).

Abraham and Moses are the best examples of this higher knowledge--besides them, who knows whether there are genuine mystics? For Philo's description of the *teleios*, the man who has become, through vision of oneness, "completely a man of God," is sometimes advanced as the ideal. Yet he can say that his own soul was "seized, as it often was, with a divine ecstasy" (*Cher.* 9). It has been said, "Philo stands alone among the writers of his time (the non-Christians at least) in having a real mystical doctrine based apparently in part at least on genuine experience" (ARMSTRONG 1947: 164).

Philo's ecstasy seems to vary between two poles. There is an ecstatic state in which the reason is caught up, and one in which the reason is completely transcended. Corresponding to this polarity is Philo's ambiguous teaching about human passion. He was faced with the conflict between Aristotelian and Stoic ethical theories, the one teaching that virtue is a mean between two vices of defect and excess, the other denying the validity of any emotion and advocating a state of *apatheia*. "By the time of Philo, the question whether

virtue means the extirpation of the emotions or only
their control seems to have been a subject of discussion among Hellenistic Jews who had a knowledge of
philosophy" (WOLFSON 1947: II.270). In general, Philo
solves the problem by accepting the Aristotelian mean
(cf *metriopatheia, Leg. All.* III.144). The majority
of men are called to eupatheia, the control of emotions
by the reason, so that "eupathy and virtue" are synon-
ymous (*Leg. All.* III.22). In this he has modified the
Stoic concept of eupathy, which was regarded as less
than virtuous (only rational apathy is truly virtue.)
Philo's eupathy is positive virtue--except for a
special class of men, the wise or enlightened, for
whom he reverts to the Stoic doctrine of apathy. For
instance, Aaron represents the Aristotelian, and Moses
the Stoic. Only Moses achieves "a complete absence of
emotion," having "the power to cut out the emotions"
including those otherwise necessary (*Leg. All.* III.128,
145, 151).

If reason and emotion are in contention for
Philo so that passion is irrational, there are nonetheless certain good emotions such as philanthropy and
pity, "a passion the most necessary and most akin to
the rational soul" (*Virt.* 18). Therefore he can present an ethical profile of the follower of Moses who
freely chooses worship, thanksgiving--especially the
spiritual *eucharistia* of the pure mind (LAPORTE;
DRUMMOND: II.301ff)--social justice, resulting in a
joy that is like a continual melody (*Somn.* 2.37; cf
Cher. 28, *Praem.* 11, *Leg. All.* II.82f). Philo is not
ascetic, although he is a strict observer of the laws
and rites of his faith, and perhaps even a puritan in
his manner of life (e.g. *Leg. All.* II.79ff, *Somn.*
II.7-9; cf LAPORTE: 191ff; DRUMMOND: II.22ff).

The richness and complexity of Philo's
thought defy systematization, and have brought the
charge of inconsistency and superficiality, "muddle-
headed and inconsistent" even though presenting some
ideas of permanent value (ARMSTRONG 1947: 161), and
"a well informed but not an original mind who has
taken many bits and pieces out of other men's systems"

(CHADWICK 1967: 155). Yet this does not measure his historical significance adequately. Philo may not have been the mystagogue that Goodenough imagined, but he is a philosopher who was able to do justice to the sense of mystery and the mystical emerging in the philosophy of his time, and to relate it positively to the Hebrew scripture.

Philo's significance for the "classical theism" of Christian historical theology involves his creation of a synthetic religious philosophy involving at least three central doctrines. First, the anonymity of God; second, the divine immutability and impassibility; third, mystical union as the way of genuine knowledge of God. His conception of the Logos is relevant at every stage, for it bears on the doctrine of the Trinity, the nature of the Incarnation, and the thorny issue of mediation in ecstatic experience. God is at rest, enjoying "perfect blessedness and happiness" beyond the motion of creatures and even the upward movement of the rational soul in search of him (*Abr.* 36). Yet he moves all things (*Fug.* 2, *Post. C.* 29f). The tension familiar in both Plato and Aristotle passes through Philo into Christian thought: how does the immoveable cause motion? and how does human being make contact with that divinity which is beyond knowledge and being? Harnack's estimate of Philo maintained that Philo's bequest was the idea that "only ecstasy produced by God himself was able to lead to the reality above reason" (HARNACK 1961: I.111f). If so, the very concept of revelation developed by the Fathers is informed largely, perhaps decisively, by the Philonic teaching. At the least, we can say that Philo represents the school-Platonism and philosophical *koinē* of his time, contributing it in the form of a religious philosophy to the Christian Fathers of the second century. They cast his thought in specifically Christian terms, of course; yet their debt to him is evident in the central conviction of classical theism, the anonymity of God and the ways of affirmation and negation that result from his namelessness.

CHAPTER 3

C L E M E N T :   T H E   T E A C H E R

(1) PHILOSOPHY AND FAITH

        Clement and Origen, the Alexandrian Fathers,
were not the first to blend philosophy with Gospel.
The Greek Apologists pioneered, and their work has a
programmatic flavor. Aristides, for instance, introduced himself as a "Christian philosopher," while
Justin Martyr even looked the part: "Justin, in
philosopher's garb, preached the word of God" (Eusebius
of Caesarea). Justin is a major figure in the story.
After making the rounds of philosophical teachers--
Stoic, Peripatetic, Pythagorean, Platonist--he was con-
verted by the witness of an old man by the seaside. His
conversion was not so contradictory as to make him de-
nounce his former quest; rather, he embraced Christianity as the true philosophy and commenced to show
the compatibility of his two loves. He commended the
Gospel to his Greek neighbours as the only safe and
profitable philosophy, indeed a search for God. Drawing
on the later Platonist speculation already examined, he
sees God as nameless, a far-off Being whom man cannot
know, describable in negations.

        Justin's teaching reflects much of the philo-
sophical theology already explored, including his own
exegetical method, which turns allegory more in the
direction of typology. His use of the Logos concept
is also a modification, in that Justin makes a thoroughgoing identification with the incarnate Christ, so that
the truth adumbrated in the philosophical idea is now
absorbed and supplanted. But again we find the typical
negative description of God, ingenerate, ineffable,
impassible, nameless. He is one of the first Christian
theologians to ask for this trouble, of relating such a
remote deity to his creation, but he does not well

appreciate what is at stake. In this regard he represents the central problem of classical theism
(GOODENOUGH 1923: 123ff; NORRIS: 41ff; CHADWICK 1966:
9ff; GILSON: 11ff).

A second figure of note in this context is
Athenagoras. He is more of an "apologist" than Justin,
defensive about the faith and not so interested in philosophy for its own sake. But he shares the same philosophical and cultural background, and his doctrine of
God draws on the common doxographical pool of opinion;
he is self-conscious about its general agreement with
his theology (e.g. *Leg.* 6). There is also the possibility of his association with Alexandria. The first
extant reference to him, by Philip of Side, deacon of
Chrysostom, states: "Athenagoras was the first head of
the school at Alexandria, flourishing in the times of
Hadrian and Antoninus, to whom also he addressed his
Legatio for the Christians; a man who embraced Christianity while wearing the garb of a philosopher, and
presiding over the academic school ... Clement, the
writer of the *Stromata*, was his pupil, and Pantaenus the
pupil of Clement" (BARNARD: 13f). The unreliability of
this historian is evident in his misunderstanding of the
relationship of Pantaenus to Clement. Yet there remains
reasonable doubt about the succession in the catechetical school, while there is other evidence, both external
and internal (e.g. the mention of camels) to support the
thesis that Athenagoras was at least acquainted with the
Alexandrian Christian community. His critical attitude
toward Greek philosophy stands in contrast to both
Justin and Clement, warning against the temptation to
simplistic assimilation.

The Greek Apologists illustrate the milieu in
which we find the great Fathers, Clement of Alexandria
and Origen. Christianity was regarded as a gnosis, a
philosophy imparted by Christ as Teacher and Illuminator.
Above all, in the doctrine of God the anonymous One,
there lies a fateful decision as preamble to theology.

46

The famous "catechetical" school in Alexandria
--probably more of a private school in the philosophical
tradition--was apparently begun by Pantaenus, a conver-
ted Stoic. This "oldest center of sacred science in the
history of Christianity" (Gilson) is characterized by
three distinctive interests, "the metaphysical investigation of the content of the faith, a leaning to the
philosophy of Plato, and the allegorical interpretation
of Sacred Scripture" (QUASTEN: II.2).

Of Pantaenus himself we know almost nothing.
One presumed fragment of his writings suggests the philosophical theology to come. He denies that God knows
intelligible things by the intellect or sensible things
by the senses; "for it is not possible that He who
transcends existences should apprehend existences by
means of existences; but we say that He knows existences
as the products of His own acts of will, adducing in
support of this a reasonable argument; for if by His
will he has created all things, to which there can be
no objection, and it is always pious and right to say
that God knows His own will, and with an act of will He
has created each thing that has been brought into existence, then it follows that God knows existences as the
products of His own acts of will, since with His will
he has created these existences" (in MOZLEY: 53). The
bare text suggests merely the familiar theme of transcendence and its relation to immanence, although the
question of God's knowing existences through his will
indicates the sort of issue which both Clement and
Origen will face in their doctrine of creation. But we
must agree with Chadwick's conclusion about Pantaenus:
"Little is known of his teaching, and it has proved a
forlorn undertaking to attempt any reconstruction of
his ideas from Clement's works" (OULTON-CHADWICK: 16).

It is Eusebius who places Clement as pupil of
Pantaenus and successor as head of the school. No
doubt there was indeed a theological "School" as tradition has it, with Pantaenus, Clement and Origen as head

at various times, and with a consistent "tradition of Christian philosophical studies" (BOUYER: 256ff). But we cannot be definite about the precise relationship among the three figures. Nor should we imagine an institutionalized School rather than a continuing catechetical *function* (DANIELOU 1955: 9ff). We know much more about Clement than about Pantaenus. Apparently raised outside the Christian faith, and probably in Athens, his search for wisdom led him to Italy, Syria and Palestine before his encounter with Pantaenus in Alexandria offered the light he sought (*Str*. i.I.11.2). His career in Alexandria spanned some twenty years, and he became head of the school probably in 200 A.D. He was forced to leave because of the persecution of Septimius Severus (Eusebius, *Hist. Eccl.* VI.6). He spent some time in Cappadocia and Antioch, his death occurring between 211 and 215.

The Christian Platonist

This "founder of speculative theology" as Quasten calls him, chose the method familiar in the philosophical schools of his day: discipline and teaching, *askēsis* and *didaskalia*, are inseparable (*Str*. ii.XVI.75.2, vi.XV.121.3). He related this to the process developed in the mysteries, a graduated discipline of initiation, training and gnosis. This process is reflected in his three great literary remains, although it seems that the third is not the *Didaskalos* which he had intended for the final stage (QUASTEN: II.12; BARDENHEWER: 50ff). Throughout his work runs a constant theme: "the true *paideia* is desire for knowledge; and the exercise (*askēsis*) of *paideia* produces love of knowledge" (vi.XV.121.3).

The first work, *Protreptikos* or 'Exhortation to the Greeks,' is an appeal "to abandon the impious mysteries of idolatry for the adoration of the divine word and God the Father." It opens with a lyrical chapter on the "New Song" of the Gospel with which

48

Clement wishes to woo his listeners away from "the bitter bondage of tyrannizing demons" (whose power lies behind the pagan myths and rites) to "the mild and loving yoke of piety." Its opening sentences, as Jaeger remarks, "have to be chanted, as was done by the New Sophists of his age, who used certain patterns of rhythmic prose" (JAEGER 1961: 132). Both form and content are geared to the office of those Exhortations down the years which aim at decision-making and acceptance of a lofty goal--the very office which Cicero's *Hortensius* would fulfil for Augustine (QUASTEN: II.8).

The second book, *Paidagōgos* or 'Tutor,' exhibits, as Clement himself states later, "the training and nurture from the state of childhood up, that is, the course of life which from elementary instruction grows by faith" (*Str.* vi.I.3). Those who heeded the initial invitation of the Logos and departed from their vain philosophy are initiated into his mystery and instructed in his wisdom. For the second stage of the *Paidagōgos* is comparable to that discipline of *catharsis* by which the initiate learns to eradicate passion and so to prepare himself for the final vision of *sacra*. It is the Christian's "lesser mysteries," like the spring initiation of the Lesser Mysteries at Agrae, preparatory to the Greater Mysteries of Eleusis in autumn. "And He, receiving you who have been trained up in excellent discipline, will teach you the oracles" (*Paed.* iii.XII.98.1; cf *Prot.* 8, 12; *Str.* v.XI.70f).

Clement's *paideia* is the work of the Logos: "Eagerly desiring then to perfect us by a gradation conducive to salvation, suited for efficacious discipline, a beautiful arrangement is observed by the all-benignant Word who first exhorts, then trains, and finally teaches" (*Paed.* i.I.3.3). The *Strōmateis* is not the *Didaskalos* to fulfil the third aim, for as its title suggests, it is a Miscellany or Patchwork (or else Tapestries, Carpets). It is a deliberate collation of various "notes," gathered from scattered and variegated flowers blooming in a meadow (*Str.* vi.I.1; cf MEHAT: 104ff for the literary genre). Perhaps some

49

of Clement's lost writings belong to this third stage--
"On First Principles," or "On the allegorical interpretation of members and affections when ascribed to God."
Or perhaps he considered the final phase to be communi-
cable rather by personal discipleship than by literary
instruction: "Our knowledge, and our spiritual garden
is the Saviour himself; into whom we are transplanted
... The Lord, then, into whom we have been transplanted,
is the Light and the true Knowledge" (*Str*. vi.I.2).

Clement's sensitivity to the "mystical" must
not be allowed to distort his method and purpose. He is
not so much a hierophant as "a fashionable lecturer,"
and in his erudition and curiosity "above all a delighted
collector" (BOUYER: I.265). His attitude toward philosophy illustrates this. He is best known as the Father
most favorably inclined to philosophy, and the exact
opposite of Tertullian's kind of exclusivism. For
scholars his writings are sources of information about
the philosophical schools of his day, the status of
leading figures and doctrines, and the positive approach
taken by a theologian anxious to provide for his faith
a proper or "scientific" basis. His is an apologetic
purpose, a fact which has been exaggerated by some commentators, especially Walther Völker, for whom Clement's
philosophical bent is preparatory and incidental (VOLKER
1952; cf DODS).. The excellent work of Salvatore Lilla
has recently surveyed "Clement's view on the Origin and
Value of Greek philosophy" and has provided a better
perspective (LILLA: 9ff; cf MOLLAND 1970: 117ff; MEHAT:
356ff). Clement advances three theories to explain the
origin of Greek philosophy: 1) the Greek philosophers
discovered some doctrines and reached certain truths by
themselves or by divine inspiration; 2) they borrowed
or stole the doctrines from the Mosaic revelation;
3) superhuman powers took philosophy from God and gave
it to men.

"The Hellenic philosophy then, according to
some, apprehended the truth accidentally, dimly, par-
tially; as others will have it, it was set going by the
devil. Several suppose that certain powers, descending

50

from heaven, inspired all philosophy. But if the Hellenic philosophy does not comprehend the whole scope of truth, and also lacks strength to perform the commandments of the Lord, yet it prepares the way for the truly royal teaching; training in some way or other, and moulding the character, and fitting him who believes in Providence (*pronoia*) for the reception of the truth" (*Str.* i.XVI.80.5f). Clement finds Greek philosophy a genuine preparation for Gospel, a kind of covenant in fact (vi.V.41f, VI.44.1). It is a *propaideia*, preparing for the "true *paideia*" which cultivates, through its own *askēsis*, the love of knowledge (vi.XV.121.3). Its attainment of truth is the result of the showering Word, raining down on men and sowing "nutritious seeds," namely the "eclectic whole" of philosophy (i.VII.37.1f). Here he repeats the theory of Philo and Justin about the Logos spreading himself over the earth like rain. But again, philosophy reflects the unity of truth: since "truth is one" the various philosophical schools "possess either no small amount or at least some part of the word of truth" for all "are illuminated by the dawning Light." Therefore, as the Bacchants severed the limbs of Pentheus, so "barbarian and Greek philosophy have torn off a piece of the eternal truth not from the mythology of Dionysos, but from the theology of the Logos who exists eternally" (*Str.* i.XIII.57.6).

Clement's is decidedly a philosophical theology. He may be called Platonist, Stoic or Eclectic; but he regards Christianity as "the true philosophy" and Platonism as the truest of Greek philosophies (*Str.* i.V.28.3, 32.4 etc.). We have mentioned his apologetic purpose. In fact he had to face two ways. To the philosopher and sceptic he must demonstrate the necessity of *faith;* to Christian obscurantists ("orthodoxasts") he must prove the connection of faith with *knowledge.* He wished to expose the fallacies and shortcomings of philosophy, while at the same time recommending its resources for Christian faith. "The problem of the reconciliation and synthesis between Christianity and Hellenism was felt by no other Christian author of the second century A.D. so deeply as by Clement. He was perfectly aware of the fact that the religion in which he firmly believed could never have become a science, or assumed the shape of a philosophical system, without taking into account the best products of Greek thought" (LILLA: 9).

Our two chief sources for Clement's attitude toward philosophy are the *Protreptikos* and the first and sixth books of Stromata. In the former treatise he exhibits breadth of learning and power of expression as he examines philosophers, poets and mysteries. His purpose is to show their grievous errors; when they do "hit on the truth" it is a sign that they are preparation for Gospel, the result of divine inspiration. He traces the philosophical quest, reaching its climax in those who looked beyond elements such as water and fire, who "sought after something higher and nobler" (5). Yet even their speculations about the Infinite (Anaximander) proved futile. At last he turns to Aristotle. Not knowing the Father of all things, he took "the Highest" to be the soul of the universe. But (the familiar charge) since he had limited the sphere of providence to the orbit of the moon and denied it to the sublunary sphere, he refutes himself, teaching that "what is without God is God."

Plato warrants a new chapter (6). In his search for truth, asks Clement, who is helper? "We do not, if you have no objection, completely disown Plato. How, then, is God to be searched out, O Plato?" There follows the *Timaeus* 28C passage, "perhaps the most hackneyed quotation from Plato in Hellenistic writers" (CHADWICK 1965: 429n; FESTUGIERE: IV.94, 271ff; STAHLIN (GCS): iv.52), and a phrase from the seventh Letter (vii.341C). Clement comments, "Well done, Plato! You have hit on the truth!" He summons Plato as guide in the investigation of the Good. For by divine inspiration certain intellects, however reluctantly, confess that "God is one, indestructible, unbegotten, and that somewhere above, in the tracts of heaven, He exists in his own appropriate eminence, truly and eternally, surveying all things." Plato especially hints at the highest truth, that God is the measure of all being: "the only just measure is the only true God, always just, continuing the self-same."

The Stromata offer ample expansion of his thesis as to the origin of Greek philosophy and its value as preparation and guide in the logic of God. He mentions the theory, taken from Jewish apologetic, that Greek philosophy has plagiarized Moses. Philosophy, indeed, may be treated under the text "All that came before Me were thieves and robbers." One must agree with what "Numenius, the Pythagorean philosopher, expressly writes: 'For what is Plato, but Moses speaking Attic Greek?'" (i.XXII.150.4). His chief theory of philosophy's rise, however, is that it is a gift of the Logos, since man exhibits a rational principle (*physikē ennoia*, i.XIX.94.2) which functions as an *eikōn* of the divine Logos (v.XIV.94.4). It is a *pneuma aisthētos* inspiring the philosophers, enabling them to grasp dimly the truth represented by the Logos (cf *Paed*. i.VI.41.3). Plato and Pythagoras, for example, "with God's help," have attained knowledge of the Mosaic truth (v.V.29.3f).

Clement's attachment to philosophy is part of his gnostic methodology too. It is not only apologetic aims that suggest a use for philosophy; the very nature of Christian truth, he claims, implies its presence in hidden dimension. "The Stromata will contain the truth mixed in the dogmas of philosophy, or rather covered over and hidden, like the edible part of the nut in the shell. For in my opinion it is fitting that the seeds of truth should be kept for the husbandman of faith, and no others" (i.I.18.1). The Gospel is a mystery, necessitating such indirection as marks the way to every secret. Clement develops a dialectical approach to God not because he is a philosopher but because in philosophy he follows Plato (cf STAHLIN (GCS) iv.50ff), convinced that truth is enigmatic, won only through the test of disciplined ascent.

53

Here is Tertullian's side of the story: "A plague on Aristotle, who taught them dialectic, the art which destroys as much as it builds, which changes its opinions like a coat, forces its conjectures, is stubborn in argument, works hard at being contentious and is a burden even to itself. For it reconsiders every point to make sure it never finishes a discussion. From philosophy come those fables and endless genealogies and fruitless questionings ... What has Jerusalem to do with Athens, the Church with the Academy, the Christian with the heretic?" (*De Praescr. Haer.* 7). Such an assessment of dialectic is at farthest remove from that of Clement. For him, both Plato and Aristotle had developed a method of knowing first principles, easily and logically extended to the Christian's knowledge of God. The two terms which operate as keys are *pistis* and *gnōsis*.

That Clement accepts the current logic of his time is evident from the eighth book of Stromata, an appendix of notes on various compendia of the day. One eclectic handbook in vogue was that of Antiochus of Ascalon, who taught that "the self-evidence of sense-perceptions represents the first, fundamental stage for the growth of knowledge and has a direct influence on reason" (LILLA: 126; cf WITT 1937: 31ff; OSBORN: 148ff). Lilla demonstrates Clement's indebtedness to this position, one which has modified both Plato and Aristotle by involving sense perception as a necessary basis. We noted earlier that Middle Platonism asserted a confidence in *archai* as trustworthy, but remained in essential agreement with the idealist epistemology of Plato. Now, however, we see that *archai* are evident to both reason and sense, an apparent compromise between rationalist and empiricist conceptualities. Such an eclectic development was already there for Clement's use.

Clement is well aware of Plato's Divided Line or fourfold division of knowledge (*Theaet.* 187ff, *Rep.*

54

vi.507a-511d; *Str.* ii.IV.13.2; CORNFORD 1935; CROMBIE:
II.1ff), but he considers sense perception as "the
ladder to knowledge." In these early chapters of Book
Two he handles the subject of "true philosophic demonstration" in a way that illustrates his homework in the
appended Book Eight. *Pistis* and *gnôsis* sustain a dual
relationship. In the first place, we give assent to
self-evident truth--either immediate knowledge or the
first principles of demonstration. Second, the results
of demonstration convict us with a form of belief.
Lilla provides a full analysis of their relationship,
as well as of another kind, assent to truths of scripture (LILLA: 119ff). In a brief article T.F. Torrance
provides helpful analysis of Clement in light of the
dichotomy (*chôrismos*) between realms of sense and intelligibility. But his neglect of those common sources
behind Clement (especially *Str.* VIII), which Lilla recognizes, modifies some of his claims regarding Clement's
"scientific" theology (TORRANCE 1966).

   Pistis means confidence in *archai* as trustworthy, axiomatic. Clement recognizes his debt to
Plato and Aristotle here (e.g. *Str.* i.XXVIII.76ff).
The "Mosaic philosophy" has four parts, the highest
being "theology, vision (*epopteia*), which Plato predicates of the truly great mysteries. And this species
Aristotle calls metaphysics. Dialectics, according to
Plato is, as he says in *The Statesman*, a science devoted to the discovery of things." Clement's "true
dialectic" is "philosophy mixed with truth," which
examines things or their essence (*ousia*), attempting
"to go beyond to the God of the universe" and professing "the science of things divine." The aim is to
isolate by analysis or abstraction "the objects of
thought," so that each will be "contemplated simply
such as it is." This is true wisdom: "the knowledge
of entities as entities." So far Clement differs
little from Plato's "hymn of dialectic" in *Rep.*
vii.532ff: the "power of dialectic" is a "discovery
of the absolute" by reason alone, in order to establish
on secure ground the first principle itself. Hence we
have Plato's propaedeutic, "all but predicting the

economy of salvation" (*Str.* v.XIV). But Plato's dialectic uses hypotheses as mere "points of departure" since the *archê* is above hypothetical knowledge, in the realm of ideas alone (*Rep.* vi.511b). It would seem that Aristotle is more relevant to Clement's argument, for the scholastic compendia on which he was drawing had accepted both Aristotle's corrections of Plato and the Peripatetic formal logic.

Aristotle had clarified the status of *archai:* "in regard to the first principles of science it is improper to ask any further for the why and wherefore of them; each of the first principles should command belief in and by itself" (*Top.* 100^b 18-21). He is distinguishing two kinds of reasoning: "demonstration" when it is from "true and primary" premises, "dialectical" when it is "from opinions that are generally accepted." Many passages, of course, bear on the matter of valid premises for syllogistic reasoning, e.g. *An Prior.* 64^bff; *An. Post.* 71^aff ("the premises of demonstrated knowledge must be true, primary, immediate ..."), 84^a29ff; *Meta.* 1011^aff; *Eth. Nic.* 1139^b26ff, 1140^b31ff. Most significant are the passages in which Aristotle defines the *archê* as indemonstrable. Thus in *Meta.* 1011^a he is scoring those pedants (such as Antisthenes?) who demand a reason for everything, seeking to demonstrate the starting-point. "But their mistake is what we have stated it to be; they seek a reason for things for which no reason can be given; for the starting-point of demonstration is not demonstration." Further, discussing the category under which to subsume the apprehension of *archai*, he concludes that "intuitive reason" grasps them, since "the first principle from which what is scientifically known follows cannot be an object of scientific knowledge, of art, or of practical wisdom; for that which can be scientifically known can be demonstrated, and art and practical wisdom deal with things that are variable" (*Eth. Nic.* 1140^b31ff; cf *An. Post.* 88^b37: "indemonstrable knowledge, which is the grasping of the immediate premise").

To the Aristotelian doctrine the Stoics added a word if not a deeper meaning: one gives *assent* (*sygkatathesis*) to primary realities (*prôta, archai*). Clement's discussion of faith as assent in the Stromata leads Henry Chadwick to remark that it "may be described as the first Christian essay in aid of a grammar of assent" (CHADWICK 1966: 51). When reason judges a certain apprehension to be true, it gives assent: "Not only the Platonists, but the Stoics, say that assent is in our power (*eph'hêmin*)" (*Str.* ii.XII.54.5). For man, Clement continues, possesses "the resources necessary for belief in the truth." Faith is a matter of choice, is indeed itself "the foundation of rational choice," not based on demonstration but a primary perception, akin to the sensation (*aisthêsis*) which Theophrastus takes as *archê* (*Str.* ii.II.9.1ff).

Wherever there is genuine knowledge, there faith is operative, for *pistis* and *gnôsis* work in tandem. "Aristotle says that the judgment which follows knowledge is indeed faith. Therefore faith is superior to knowledge, and is its criterion" (*Str.* ii.IV.15.5—a play on words, *kyriôteron* and *kritêrion*). The two functions or forms of faith—"the faith of knowledge and the faith of opinion"—correspond to twofold demonstration (ii.XI.48.1). The latter refers to the two sorts of syllogism which Aristotle distinguished (e.g. *Top.* 100ª, 22-31), namely scientific syllogism and dialectical (or rhetorical) syllogism. The distinction between *epistêmê* and *doxa* recalls Plato's dichotomy, but whereas he restricted genuine knowledge to the world of intelligibles, Aristotle based his distinction on the validity or invariability of the premises. Clement's discussion in Book Eight suggests his familiarity with these logical technicalities. In chapter III (viii.5.1ff) demonstration is carefully defined over against both *syllogism*, by which he means the dialectical-rhetorical kind based on opinion rather than true premises, and *analysis*, the relating of conclusions to first principles. But he recognizes that "demonstration" is often referred less strictly to that argument based on opinion and aimed at "persuasion merely." His own discussion (or that of the handbook behind it) turns precisely on the Aristotelian distinctions. As against the uncertainty of mere syllogisms involving multiple stages of logic, there is the strict demonstration, beginning with that self-evident or indemonstrable premise which has the capacity to encourage belief: "from points already believed to be capable of producing belief in what is not yet believed" (7.6).

Clement's aim in all this is to show "the method of discovery" (*methodos tês heureseôs*, 9.6). He is consistent throughout the Stromata in taking theology as inquiry, a search for or way of discovering truth; Book Eight indeed begins with a chapter extolling the true or Barbarian philosophy for its commitment to inquiry—seek, knock and ask (*Matt.* vii.7). To questioners, Clement continues, God will give "knowledge, by way of comprehension, through the true illumination of logical investigation" (viii.I.2; cf vi.XV.121.4 for the connection between inquiry and discovery, *zêtêsis* and *heuresis*; also CAMELOT: 56ff). Theology is thus a heuristic enterprise, using philosophical tools such as logic to assure itself of a proper process of investigation, confident that God stands behind all truth and rewards those who seek in a true manner. The two forms of *pistis* merge in this properly theological inquiry, since Scripture is a sort of *archê* which provides further demonstration. "Therefore, as is reasonable, grasping by faith the indemonstrable first principle, and receiving in abundance, from the first principle itself, demonstrations in reference to the first principle, we are by the voice of the Lord trained up (*paideuometha*) to the knowledge of the truth" (*Str.* vii.XVI.95.6).

Demonstration with Scripture as base is the way to criticize various opinions, especially those termed heresies (*Str.* vii.XV.92.3). Thus a truly theological *apodeixis* results, leading to what Clement calls a rational faith, *epistêmonikê pistis* (e.g.

Str. ii.XI.49.3, viii.III.5.3). Such faith is the
same as *gnôsis*, the "knowledge of the thing in itself,
or the knowledge which harmonizes with what takes
place" (*Str.* ii.XVII.76.3). Belief and knowledge,
Clement says at one point (iv.XXII.143.2f) derive from
the same word, *stasis*: *epistêmê* means that the mind
(*psychê*) is no longer vacillating but "settles in objects," while faith similarly refers to the "settling
of our mind respecting that which is." To take one's
stand in what truly is, what has really happened, recalls Philo's doctrine of the faithful man as one
given a place to stand by the God who is immoveable.
The concepts of immutability and impassibility are
never far from this logical model of Clement's. Faith
is a way, we might say, between a preconception or
hope (*prolêpsis*) and an activity or vocation. The
Christian gnostic begins, as every learner does, from
a proleptic concept of truth (ii.IV.16.3, 17.1ff), a
desire to know (cf LILLA: 129f and CAMELOT: 29ff for
the Epicurean and Stoic notion of prolepsis).

Clement's dialectic, then, is linked with
his philosophical or logical heritage, but also with
his gnostic interpretation of the Christian revelation. We have seen that knowledge is a kind of faith,
rational or scientific faith. In *Str.* vii.X he defines gnosis as the perfecting of faith, a developing
"to be acquired as far as possible." "Faith is then,
so to speak, a comprehensive knowledge of the essen-
tials; and knowledge is the strong and sure demonstration of what is received by faith" (57.3). It leads
to love, to the "right action" of the gnostic way of
life. Such gnostic faith reflects what Harry Wolfson
calls the "double faith theory," originating in
Aristotle but first applied theologically by Clement.
Wolfson considers the faith which is *doxastikê* as a
"short-cut," while that which is *epistêmonikê* is the
proper form. This may be contrasted with Origen's
view that despite the wide difference between simple
faith and faith conjoined with knowledge, the term
"retains for him that single meaning of acceptance"
(WOLFSON 1956: 109, 120ff; but cf KIRK: 314).

Is every man of faith a "gnostic" for Clement? Sometimes it seems so, inasmuch as he calls faith the "criterion" of knowledge (ii.IV.15.5). But to take this passage out of context would be to mis-interpret Clement's doctrine, as Gilson has done: "he means to say that all the Christians are the true Gnostics." Gilson's preconception of the role of philo-sophy as handmaid puts him in favour of Clement. Thus he can qualify his thesis by stating that some Chris-tians "are the only Gnostics worthy of the name," and even reject it: "Not every Christian is a 'Gnostic', because not all have knowledge, but all true Gnostics are Christians; the true Gnostic is the Christian per-fect in knowledge" (GILSON: 30, 33, 569a). Lilla pre-sents a more satisfactory account, concluding that "Clement's conception of *pistis* and of its relations with *gnôsis* is a perfectly coherent doctrine," because of the two meanings of faith, a simple and a scienti-fic one, noted above (LILLA: 141). The kind of faith intended here is that advanced, rational or scientific *pistis* that comes by rational demonstration from the *archê* of Scripture. His debt to Philo throughout this topic is evident. He steers a Philonic course in his illustration of philosophy's role as handmaid of theology; a further step on this way is taken as he repeats the idea of the higher student, the gnostic believer who penetrates beyond the literal meaning to the symbolic, and beyond the bodily sphere of vocation to that passionless imitation of God which marks true likeness.

Abstract Theology

        Clement's "true dialectic," or "real philo-sophy and true theology" (*Str.* v.IX.56.3), identifies the true philosophical approach to the One of Middle Platonism with the theological approach to the God of the biblical revelation. He had worked his way through the complexities of formal logic, with its distinctions in the language of attribution and the classification

of categories and terms, including the familiar univo-
city, equivocity and analogy (viii.VIII.23). He had
also studied the myths of Plato, acknowledging the hermeneutical task involved (iv.XXIII.147.1; cf v.XII.78
on *Tim.* 28C). And he appreciated the philosopher's
intention in the mythological passages. "Rightly,
then, Plato, in the Letters, treating of God, says:
'We must speak in enigmas ... ' For the God of the
universe, who is above all speech, all conception,
all thought, can never be committed to writing, being
inexpressible (*arrêtos*) even by his own power" (*Str.*
v.X.65.1f). This statement is in the context of a
lengthy discussion of the poets and philosophers, who
used symbols and enigmas as helps to "right theology
and piety" (chapts. VI-IX).

His understanding of the role of symbols
parallels Plato's theory of myths. There is first
the stage when the initiate must pass from the sensible
to the intelligible realm. The *encyclia* of classical
education--dialectics, astronomy, geometry--are the
means for this stage, since they confront us with the
changeless (geometry), the higher cosmic harmony
(astronomy) and intelligibles (dialectics)(LILLA:
169ff). Such approach to the intelligible realm
(*noêta*) leaves behind that common sort of knowledge,
improperly so called, which sticks at sense perception.
For the true knowledge "bears the impress of judgment
and reason, in the exercise of which there will be
rational cognitions alone, applying purely to the objects of thought, and resulting from the bare energy
of the mind" (*Str.* vi.I.3.2). This Platonic ideal of
contemplation will involve a method of abstraction appropriate to the pure intelligibility of the goal, and
the ineffability ascribed to it.

The eleventh chapter of *Str.* v (71.2ff) contains Clement's explicit meditation on this method.
What constitutes the acceptable sacrifice to God is
"unswerving abstraction from the body and its passions."
Philosophy is the practice of death, for one must deny
himself all use of the senses: only he that "with

pure mind itself applies to objects, practises the true philosophy." Thus Pythagoras prescribed for his disciples five years of silence, so that in abstraction from objects of sense "they might with the mind alone contemplate the Deity." Clement suggests that a two-fold method is demanded by this understanding of abstractions, "purification by confession" and "contemplation by analysis," corresponding to the minor mysteries of the faith (71.2).

The Christian gnostic will proceed by the method of abstraction in seeking knowledge of the divine attributes. He will not "imagine that hands, and feet, and mouth, and eyes, and entrance and exit, and jealousies and threats, are said by the Hebrews to be attributes of God." These are "used more piously in an allegorical sense" which he will describe in due time. But first Clement wishes to clarify his method. The analysis of reality means the elimination of *all* properties, "abstracting from the body its physical properties, taking away the dimension of depth, then that of breadth, and then that of length. For the point which remains is a unit (*monas*), so to speak, having position; from which if we abstract position (*thesis*), there is the conception of unity." This Euclidean method, already familiar in Middle Platonism as we have seen, becomes for Clement the way to the highest knowledge of God. "If, then, abstracting all that belongs to bodies and things called incorporeal, we cast ourselves into the magnitude (*megethos*) of Christ, and thence advance into the immensity (*achanēs*) by holiness, we may reach somehow to the conception of the Almighty, knowing not what he is, but what he is not." For he is the First Cause above space, time, name and conception--in that realm "which Plato called the region of ideas."

In the following Chapter (v.XII.78ff) Clement pursues the logic of his argument. God is declared to be ineffable: "invisible and unutterable (*aoratos esti kai arrētos*) ... what is divine is unutterable

62

(*aphthegton*) by human power." Drawing on favorite
Scripture texts (*I. Cor.* 2:6f, *Col.* 2:2f) he describes
Christian truth as a mystery, hidden in the parabolic
speech of Christ, inasmuch as "the truly sacred mystic
word, respecting the unbegotten and his powers, ought
to be concealed." How fitting then, according to
Clement, that St. John should describe "invisibility
and ineffability" as the Father's bosom (John 1:8).
But Clement thinks it appropriate also that "some have
called it the Depth (*Bythos*), as containing and emboso-
ming all things, inaccessible and boundless" (81.3).

Here Clement pauses for breath. "This discourse respecting God is most difficult to handle."
For every first principle is "hard to discover," and
how much more "the absolutely first and oldest principle?" God is "neither genus, nor difference, nor
species, nor individual, nor number." He is All and
Father, indivisible and infinite--the latter most sig-
nificantly, "not considered with reference to inscruta-
bility, but with reference to its being without dimensions, and not having a limit." Therefore it is form-
less and nameless. When we name God (One, Good, Father,
God, Creator) we do so *improperly*. "We speak not as
supplying His name; but for lack, we use good names,
in order that the mind may have these as points of
support, so as not to err in other respects. For each
one by itself does not express God; but all together
are indicative of the power of the Omnipotent."

This statement, reflecting as it does the
common wisdom of Middle Platonism, illustrates sharply
the problem of the Alexandrian view of transcendence.
Once the mind has pressed abstraction to its limit,
understanding what God is not, what remains for significant utterance? Plotinus, quite logically, will
introduce his category of ecstasy at this critical
point. Clement relies on his doctrine of the Logos:
"It remains that we understand, then, the Unknown,
by divine grace, and by the word alone that proceeds
from Him."

(2) *WITHOUT MOTION OR EMOTION*

Clement and Origen, like Philo before them, preserved the transcendence of God only by a radical separation of the One from the "many" of the world. "The very gods of Epicurus, living their blissful lives apart, without care or concern for the affairs of the lower world, are not more cut off and unrelated than this lonely unit, which is the ultimate term of abstract thinking" (TOLLINTON 1932: 36). In this sense they stand in utter contradiction to *anthropomorphic* conceptions of deity. Their intent was also to safeguard the idea of God from the taint of responsibility for evil, a kind of theodicy. In this respect they stand opposed also to *anthropopathic* conceptions of deity. The unity and relationship of these two problematic conceptions, anthropomorphism and anthropopathism, and the Alexandrian solution, pose a question. Do not Clement and Origen, in thus purifying their idea of God, enervate their christology of its genuinely soteriological element? Moreover, since 'like knows like' in the Alexandrian worldview, the doctrine of man implies a similar attribution of negative qualities: "the way to the Immutable is by immutability (*pros to atrepton ... atreptō*)" (*Str.* ii.XI.51.6). Thus the question about christology is joined to the question about anthropology, and the crucial link is that of the particular humanity which Logos assumed.

The Image of God: the Logos

Clement's discovery that God remains essentially unknowable except as an implication of dialectical abstraction does not lead to despair, because the Logos or Son remains knowable in himself; and in himself he is the image of God. "God, then, not being subject to demonstration, is not an object of knowledge. But the Son is wisdom and knowledge and truth, and all else that has affinity thereto. He is also susceptible of demonstration and of description. And all the powers of the Spirit, becoming collectively one thing, terminate in the same point--that is, in the Son ... He is the circle of all powers rolled and united into one unity" (*Str.* iv.XXV.156). This Pythagorean mode of statement suggests the kind of absolute place which the Logos holds, akin to Philo's doctrine. All the divine powers are subsumed under the power and being of the Logos; He is their fullness.

The Christian gnostic ascends from intellectual ideas to "what is oldest in origin, the timeless and unoriginated First Principle and Beginning of existences--the Son." From the Son one learns of "the remoter Cause, the Father of all things, most ancient and most beneficent of all; not capable of expression by voice, but to be adored with reverence and silence and holy wonder, and supremely venerated; declared by the Lord, as far as those who learned were capable of comprehending, and understood by those chosen by the Lord to respond" (*Str.* vii.I.3). It is by "becoming the Gospel" that the Word breaks "the mystic spell of the prophetic enigmas" (*Prot.* I.10.1).

Clement can speak in rich and exalted language about the nature of the Logos. He occupies "the highest preeminence" above all angelic beings, for the Father has subjected "the whole army of angels and gods" to His administration (*Str.* vii.II.5). He never moves from his "watchtower" (a simile from Plato), yet exists everywhere free from limitations. As the "power" of the Father, it is upon Him that all creation gazes, "the supreme Administrator of the universe, as he pilots all in safety according to the Father's will, rank being subordinated to rank under different leaders, till in the end the great High Priest is reached." His salvation comes upon all ranks "by the initiation and through the instrumentality of One." Another passage refers to Christ as "both the foundation and the superstructure ... Now the extremes, i.e., the beginning and the end, I mean faith and love, are not matters of teaching; but knowledge ..." (vii.X.55). Such a total view of mediation by the Logos is cast in terms very close to that of Christian Gnosticism.

Valentinus, most important of the Gnostic teachers and chief target for the polemic of Irenaeus, is quoted six times by Clement. Clement's familiarity with the Valentinian gnosis is clear from his *Excerpta ex Theodoto*, a scrapbook of notes and comments, although the substance of his own critique is hard to distinguish from Theodotos (see F. Sagnard's introduction to SC 23, pp 21ff). Born in Egypt, Valentinus had been educated in Alexandria before removing to Rome. His doctrine of God involves the highly speculative concept of *Plêrôma*, the habitation of the highest spirits. These are arranged as a hierarchy of Aeons, descending from the supreme deity, *Bythos* or Abyss. Grouped in pairs (syzygies), the primary Ogdoad consists of Abyss and Silence (*Sigê*), from whom emanate Mind and Truth, and so come Word and Life, then Man and Church. The lowest reach of the Pleroma is the final aeon, Sophia. It is her unbridled desire to procure a vision of Abyss that leads to her fall, and the production of Demiurgus and the matter from which he made the world. It is the fallen Sophia that is the object of the Redeemer's work, a reconciliation within the Pleroma itself. The procession of a new pair of aeons, Christ and Holy Spirit, brings the redemption into the created order as a way of escape into the higher realm of true being.

Gnosticism was as concerned with the problem of mediation as were Clement and Origen, and as convinced that the solution was to be found in a doctrine of redemptive spiritual intermediaries. But the Gnostic emanation of aeons from the Abyss is different in kind from the Fathers' doctrine of Logos. Their Logos Christology begins not in a Pleroma out of Abyss, but in God the Father; it ends, not in the theophany of an eternal aeon, but in the incarnation of the heavenly Son. Yet often the issues were not so clearly stated in this ante-Nicene theological climate. Both Clement and Origen speak easily of the Father as Abyss. Both can say that there is a divine Silence which is closer to the Abyss than is the uttered Word. Both are hesitant to admit as ontological fact any change or "passion" in divinity, as incarnation seems to imply.

Both are anxious to preserve the truth of "gnosticism"
--a philosophical interpretation of mythology, and an
insistence that gnosis originates in divine gift
(*charis*) and issues in mystic union.

The tension of his gnosticism is seen most
clearly in Clement's treatment of the humanity of
Jesus. His concern for the incarnate Logos is a striking modification of his Platonic philosophy, yet in
turn his christology is conditioned by his concept of
impassibility. As the Word is the image of God, he
mirrors that which is distinctively divine, namely
impassibility; "the image of God is the divine and
royal Word, the impassible man (*anthrôpos apathês*)"
(*Str.* v.XIV.94.5).

The "Entirely Impassible" Christ

The question before Clement is this: since
by definition God is not, while man is, subject to
emotion, how can Logos experience genuine incarnation?
Clement is quite clear in his premises. "God is
impassible, free of anger, destitute of desire. And
He is not free of fear, in the sense of avoiding what
is terrible; or temperate, in the sense of having
command of desires. For neither can the nature of God
fall in with anything terrible, nor does God flee fear;
just as He will not feel desire, so as to rule over desires" (*Str.* iv.XXIII.151.1ff). Man, on the other
hand, possesses "flesh with its capacity for suffering
... by nature subject to passion" (*Str.* vii.II.6, 7).

In describing the life of the gnostic (*Str.*
vii) Clement stresses the divine impassibility to such
a degree that it appears quite incapable of any property of grace. He seeks to show the superiority of
Christian gnosticism by proving the purity of its idea
of God. For the gnostic is master of "divine science,"
the function of which is "to investigate the First
Cause and that through which all things were made,"
as well as virtue and vice and the acquisition of

wisdom. In chapter IV he turns to the proper description of deity. The Greeks "assume their gods to be
human in passions as they are human in shape; and,
as each nation paints their shape after its own likeness (according to the saying of Xenophanes, the
Ethiopians black with turned up nose, the Thracians
with red hair and blue eyes), so each represents them
as like itself in soul." Even Greeks, though milder
than barbarians, make their gods subject to passion.
Only the gnostic, "truly royal in soul," knows that
God is "alone meant to be honored and revered, alone
glorious and beneficent, abounding in well-doing, the
author of all good and of nothing that is evil" (22).
The beginning of truth therefore lies in "cleansing
our souls from bad and wicked opinions by means of
right reason," in order to turn to "more excellent
principles." Clement finds this to be parallel to the
mystery cults, in which the initiate must be purified
"before the communication of the mysteries" (27).

          Clement now is able to advance to Christian
truth: "we refuse to circumscribe in a given place
him who is incomprehensible, and to confine in temples
made with hands that which contains all things" (V.1).
For the "self-existent Deity" needs not such things
as man requires. If any creature is "holy" it is the
Church ("I use the name of Church now not of the place,
but of the congregation of saints"), and especially the
gnostic, in whom we find "the likeness, the divine and
sanctified image." Moreover, as God is not "made like
the form of any creature," so "neither is he of like
passions" (VI.1). For "things that are capable of suffering are all mortal." Therefore the idea of God is
understood rightly only when freed from such limitations. He need not be in human shape in order to hear,
for instance--"God is all ear and all eye, if one may
make use of these expressions" (VII.37). It is this
attribution of such properties as omnipresence that
allows the gnostic to worship in every place and at
any time.

The key to Clement's theology is his doctrine of the likeness between the gnostic and the Logos—and the likeness consists in impassibility (STAHLIN (GCS): iv.252). Clement, however, will not deny the reality of the Incarnation: he cannot lightly be charged with docetic heresy. He can pray, "Sympathize with us; for you know from your own suffering (*autopathōs*) the weakness of the flesh" (*Paed*. 1.VIII.62.2). He can say that the Word is loving because God is loving, and that it is the Lord who suffered for us, whom he might have destroyed. He can say, "it was not without the wood that he came to our knowledge" (*Str*. v.XI.72.3). There is also the famous passage in his sermon on riches (*Q.D.S*. 37.2): "God himself is love and was revealed because of love. In his unspeakable greatness lies his Fatherhood. In his fellowship with our experience is Motherhood. The Father takes a woman's nature in his love ... " A fragment from a homily on Luke 15 echoes the theme: "What choral dance and high festival is held in heaven" at the return of a prodigal; "the kind Father" is "moved with compassion" (ANF II.581, Frag. XI). At one point he can put it starkly: "the God who suffered" (*Prot*. 106.4), although this early formulation is left behind by the time he composes the Stromata. All this follows from Clement's insistence that God is active love; his immutability means, as it did for Philo, that He "continues immutably in the self-same goodness" (*Str*. vi.XII.104.3). Thus he writes that "he alone is the true God who is unchangeably the same in his just beneficence " (vii.III.15). His providence arises "from pity of our weakness ... like the care of shepherds for their sheep and that of a king toward his subjects" (vii.XII.42).

It is perhaps strange that Clement comes so close to the notion of *sympatheia* familiar in Stoicism and in concert with astralism and other features of the classical world-view (MACGREGOR-PURDY: 291ff; ANGUS: 117ff). Stranger, perhaps, that he does not cast this notion in stronger terms when he suggests a passion of God in the form of incarnate Logos. Probably he is too well aware of the pantheism lurking

69

behind the Stoic *sympatheia tôn holôn*, or the popular superstition (still with us in technological society!) about the astrological "correspondences" of the mimetic universe, and the endless ways of putting them to practical use. The Platonic *mimêsis* offered Clement a safer model because it posited the archetypal patterns in a strictly noetic world--a "relaxed dualism" compatible with the "relaxed monism" of the biblical tradition (HENRY: xl).

The idea of accommodation is present in this element of Clement's thought. Discussing the propriety of speaking of divine "anger," he remarks that even this "passion" is full of love to man, "God condescending to emotion on man's account; for whose sake also the Word of God became man" (*Paed.* i.VIII. 74.4). There follows (IX.75ff) an analysis of "the mode of his loving pedagogy," in which "the Lord acts toward us as we do toward our children." Yet such *katabasis* exhausts itself in the act of incarnation itself, in the role of teacher and exemplar assumed by the Word. His incarnational suffering is not essential to that role, for it is undesigned by God. His will extends only to that which is good, and suffering (as the Platonic theory taught) is a good only when it is punitive or corrective. Since neither category applies to the sinless Christ, his suffering is accidental to the divine condescension and salvation (cf *Str.* iv.XXIV.153f).

Thus the Christian is called to believe "that He is the Son, and that He came, and how, and for what, and respecting His passion" (*Str.* v.I.2); and yet is called also to understand these things according to their "higher" meaning. In a section treating the scriptures that ascribe human affections to God (*Str.* ii.XVI.72ff), Clement warns against beginning from our own affections, and so interpreting "the will of the impassible deity similarly to our perturbations." For the divine being "cannot be declared as it exists: but as we who are fettered in the flesh were able to hear, so the prophets spoke to us; the Lord in a saving way accommodating (*symperiphero-menou*) Himself to the weakness of men." It is *our* joy that God appropriates to Himself, for instance: "so He rejoices, without suffering change, by reason of him who has repented being in joy, as he willed." And of the Incarnation ("manifest mystery: God in man and man God") he can state that "the compassionate God himself freed the flesh" (*Paed.* iii.I, 2.1, 3).

Clement's theology, therefore, seems caught in definitions which limit the historical significance of the Incarnation--a noetic redemption dangerously akin to Gnosticism. The Gnostic Gospel was the good news that Jesus had appeared in order to instruct a chosen few in esoteric doctrine. Clement's Christian *paideia* assigns to Christ the role of Teacher, leading his pupils through stages of understanding toward that perfection reserved for the gnostic who imitates and participates in his own wisdom (e.g. *Paed.* i.I.6, V.12, *Str.* v.I.3f, IX.56f). His didactic role thus limits the work of Christ and raises the most serious question about Clement's christology.

Incarnation: history or parable?

It would seem that Clement provides solid evidence for taking the historicity of the Incarnation most seriously (CASEY: 63). "The Saviour comes to us himself and suffers on our account, running his human course from birth to the cross" (*Q.D.S.* 8.2). "Now the Word issuing forth (*proelthōn*) was the cause of creation; then also he generated himself, when the Word became flesh, that he might be seen" (*Str.* v.III.16.5). In *Str.* vii.II he describes the Teacher who is both Son of God and Saviour of men: "he who for our sake took upon him our flesh with its capacity for suffering" (6.5); "he had taken upon him our flesh" (7.5); "he scorned not the weakness of human flesh, but having clothed himself with it, has come into the world for the common salvation of men" (8.1). Such "clothing with flesh" (*sarkophoros, Str.* v.VI.34.1) is so real that Clement can speak of "the blood of the Word," and of being "swathed in his precious blood" (*Paed.* i.VI.40.2ff; iii.III.25.2).

In a passage that seems decisive (*Str.* v.XV.127) he states: "the whole economy which prophesied of the Lord appears indeed a parable to those who know not the truth, when one speaks and the rest hear that the Son of God--of Him who made the universe--assumed flesh, and was conceived in the virgin's womb (as his material body was produced) and subsequently, as was the case, suffered and rose again ... But on the scriptures being opened up, and declaring the truth to those who have ears, they proclaim the very suffering endured by the flesh, which the Lord assumed, to be · 'the power and wisdom of God'." Again, "those who consider themselves wise deem it mythical (*mythôdes*) that the Son of God should speak through a man, and that God should have a Son, and especially that the Son should have suffered" (*Str.* i.XVIII.88.5). He can also wax lyrical about the theme: "O divine mystery! ... O mystic wonder ! The Lord was laid low, and man rose up ..." (*Prot.* XI.111.3).

The *parousia* of the Saviour (*Str.* i.XVIII.88.6) proves a scandal and a fable because man's preconceived notion (*prolêpsis*) inclines him to a false expectation in regard to God. This question of what is appropriate to deity (*theoprepês*) will concern us in the final chapter. Here we should note Clement's struggle to develop a doctrine of God appropriate to the event of the Incarnation. Since the christological controversies still lay ahead, he cannot be expected to raise those questions which would form the classic problematic for the Chalcedonian formula. He operates in a simpler framework, and offers a simpler model of a divine-human union, a historical event which constitutes a *mystery* (*Prot.* III, XI, *Paed.* iii.I.2.1, etc; FLOYD: 75ff). Yet he is sure that the docetism of the Gnostics represents a fatal error, in minimizing the significance of flesh, particularly as manifested in marriage. Thus he attacks--in *Str.* iii where the subject is marriage--

Marcion (III.12, IV.25), Tatian (VI.49, XII.81f),
Cassianus (XIII.91) and Gnostics in general (e.g. VII.60:
"those who from a hatred for the flesh ungratefully long
to have nothing to do with the marriage union and the
eating of reasonable food, are both blockheads and
atheists, and exercise an irrational chastity like the
other heathen").

Clement's intention seems clear; he wants to
honor the Incarnation as an assumption of true flesh, a
genuine *katabasis* of divine love (e.g. *Q.D.S.* 37.1f,
Str. v.VI.38.6, XIV.105.4 - GRILLMEIER: 161). At the
beginning of *Str.* v (on faith and its mysteries) there
occurs a significant passage. Whereas, states Clement,
some draw a distinction "that faith refers to the Son,
and knowledge to the Spirit," "in order to believe
truly in the Son, we must believe that he is the Son,
and that he came, and how, and for what, and respecting
his passion" (I.2). It soon becomes clear that he has
in mind Basilides and Valentinus, who rely on natural
or aesthetic modes of salvation, "apart from the presence of the Saviour" (*tou sôtêros parousia*, 3.3).
This error ignores the fact of providence (*pronoia*)
which governs and guarantees the divine economy (6.2).
Now it is necessary to acknowledge Clement's emphasis
on the true sufferings of Christ, and the fact that he
follows the radical logic of *katabasis* as descent even
into hell (FLOYD: 81). Thus Christ experienced genuine
pain as a sacrificial offering for sin (e.g. *Str.*
v.XI.70, X.66.5). But it is pressing Clement's doctrine too far to translate *Str.* v.I.1.2 (*peri tou
pathous*) as "*respect* his passion" (FLOYD: 75), as if
Clement is making a point about taking Christ's passion with a special seriousness. He is doing that, of
course, insofar as his polemic with Gnostic docetism
requires it. But what is surely decisive is the question whether Clement's own gnosticism is able to
sustain this seriousness in the long run. How far
does *he* go "respecting his passion?"

Our critique of Clement's christology is
based on two sorts of data, both stemming from his

epistemology. He is explicit about accepting the
theory of knowledge which makes a sharp separation
(*chōrismos*) between two realms or two worlds, *kosmos
noētos* and *kosmos aisthētos*: "the world of thought
and the world of sense--the former archetypal, and the
latter the image of that which is called the model"
(*Str.* v.XIV.93.4ff; cf iv.XXIII.148.1 on sensible and
intellectual objects; vi.I.3.1 on two modes of knowing;
also MEIFORT: 13ff). The typical Pythagorean and
Platonic epistemology had profound consequences
for classical anthropology. The gap between appearance
and reality, sense and intellect, matter and mind, is
familiar as the ontological separation which haunts
every idealism, and which so often leads to an abandonment of the material pole in favor of the survival of
the mental. The problem is ignorance; the solution is
education.

Clement's theology is a Christian *paideia*.
Christ is the Teacher, who educates man by training his
soul to discover truth (e.g. *Str.* iv.VI.35.1, vi.XV.121,
vii.XVI.95.6--all forms of the verb *paideuo*; cf STAHLIN
(GCS) iv.616 for *paideia*). The title and theme of his
Paedagōgos reflects the same stance. "Paedagogy is the
training of children ... we are the children" (i.V.12.1);
"To speak briefly, the Lord acts toward us as we do toward our children" (i.IX.75.1). Moreover, it may be
significant that Clement's design in the three chief
works moves from the proclamation of atonement (*Prot.*)
through the description of divine paideia (*Paed.*) to
the analysis of intellectual faith (*Str.*). Now there
are texts which suggest adherence to the "classic"
theory of atonement (FLOYD: 82f; e.g. *Prot.* 111.2:
"He subdued the serpent and enslaved the tyrant death;"
cf *Paed.* iii.2.3; 85.1; *Str.* ii.X.47.3; iv.VII.51.1).
Yet once again the wider context and the ultimate intention raise questions. It is not that Clement accepts
the Gnostic doctrine that matter is evil, birth a fall
into prison, and salvation an escape through immateria-
lity--he scores all this in *Str.* vii.III.13 for instance.
Rather, his theory of the two realms drives a wedge
between the Saviour's historical work and his ultimate

role as Teacher. In a striking metaphor, history has become "a vast spiral" related to the historical Jesus as to a new axis (MONDESERT: 188). We should recall that every text has two meanings (*Str*. vi.XV.126ff), a lower and a higher. Faith is the grasp of higher meanings, and the Christian a gnostic who attains this right interpretation. The hermeneutical process reflects Clement's intellectualism, and bears on his soteriology.

The famous allegorical method of interpretation is on display in a passage (*Str*. v.VI.37-40) which underlines the question at issue. Clement calls it "the mystical interpretation" (*tēn mystikēn hermēneian*). Israel's high priest used to put on a special garment reserved for entry into the Holy of Holies. Now the robe is "symbol of the world of sense," and type of the incarnation. For after his suffering, Christ puts off the robe of sense, washing it away in order to enter the realm of intelligibles. He put on the economy of salvation like a garment, and on reentering the noetic realm put it off. "Now the Lord, having come alone into the noetic world enters by his sufferings (*dia tōn pathōn*), introduced into the knowledge of the ineffable." His conclusion is twofold: "in one way, I think that the Lord puts off and puts on by descending into the region of sense; and in another, he who believes through him puts off and puts on the consecrated stole, as the apostle suggested" (40.3). Thus the *pronoia* behind the *oikonomia* turns out to be a function of the noetic world, overcoming the fall into the sensible world by a *parousia* which may take real flesh and experience real sufferings, but which is an appearance soon to be removed for reentry into the true world (TORRANCE 1966: 231ff).

Is this a fair summary of Clement's doctrine? It is if one considers the idea which reinforces it, impassibility. In the very passages where he insists on the reality of incarnation, Clement describes the flesh which the Logos assumed in terms that reveal a christology as questionable as that of Docetism. In *Str*. iii.II.6-10 God is defined as "eternally free from passion" and man "subject to passion." Now "after he

had taken upon him our flesh, which is by nature subject to passion, he trained it to a habit of impassibility." This *hexis apatheias* recalls the definition
of deity, and of the imitation of God. Clement is pro-
posing the thesis that the incarnate Logos perfects
man in the likeness of passionless deity, making Incarnation an instrumental function of the escape from
flesh, and not the redemption of flesh itself. The
issue is even sharper in other passages, where Clement's
shorthand definition of Christ is: "He was entirely
impassible" (*hapaxaplōs apathēs ēn* - *Str*. vi.IX.71.2).
The context here is the insistence that the gnostic
Christian is subject only to necessary bodily functions
such as eating and drinking. But in the case of Christ,
Clement points out, "it were ludicrous (to suppose)
that the body, as body, demanded the necessary aids in
order to survive. For he ate, not for the sake of the
body, which was kept together by a holy energy, but in
order that it might not enter into the minds of those
who were with him to entertain a different opinion of
him." Christ ate and drank not because he needed to
but to prevent our *thinking* that he did *not* need to!

Christ's eating and drinking bothers Clement
in another place (*Str*. iii.VII.59.3). Here he quotes
with approval a letter of Valentinus to Agathopus:
"Jesus endured all things and was continent; it was his
endeavor to earn a divine nature; he ate and drank in
a manner peculiar to himself, and the food did not
pass out of his body. Such was the power of his con-
tinence that food was not corrupted within him; for he
himself was not subject to the process of corruption."
This theory is consistent with Valentinus' own tri-
partite anthropology, according to which Christ's was
a "psychic" body on the way to being perfectly "pneumatic" (e.g. *Str*. iii.XVII.102.3). Clement can call
Christ's descent into the flesh a kind of "sleep-
walking" (*Str*. v.XIV.105.2f). Again, he was "no
ordinary man that he should also be in need of some
helpmeet after the flesh" (*Str*. iii.VI.49.3).

76

The evidence suggests an uneven attempt to engage in two separate battles, with both those extreme Gnostics who denied the goodness of the created order, symbolized by marriage, and those who took Christ too lightly, identifying him as an ordinary mortal. Clement's polemic against the Gnostics insists on the reality of the incarnation, the truth of the redemptive events of assumption of flesh, sufferings and death. Yet he seems to give the game away in other contexts when in unequivocal terms he insists that Christ's flesh was special, his body functioning in a peculiar way (*idiôs*), appearing to be truly human only to counteract the heresy of docetism ("appearance"). Now scholars have commented on this issue. "It is true that Clement has repeatedly been suspected of docetism, but he consistently maintains the reality of the human nature of Christ, though at the same time his tendency to spiritualize seems to make the reality of the Incarnation merely relative" (GRILLMEIER: 161). There is a "distinctly docetic ring" about his christology, the "problematical element" of which "springs from the way he allowed it to be colored by the Greek ascetical ideal of *apatheia*, or emancipation from passion" (KELLY: 154). Again, despite certain "meagre and unsatisfactory" aspects, Clement's "idea of the Saviour is larger and nobler--may we say less conventional?--than that of any other doctor of the church" (BIGG: 103; cf FLOYD: 78, CAMELOT: 80f, CHADWICK 1966: 50f).

Clement's doctrine of impassibility, therefore, informs the range of his anthropology and theology. Likeness to God means an image of *apatheia*, even if, as R.M. Grant points out, man cannot attain the perfection of the divine *apatheia* so that there remains an "absolute differentiation" between God and man (R.M. GRANT 1966: 113). It could be said that his understanding of the incarnation of the Word is that it is truly historical, a genuine assumption of humanity, but that his definition of humanity is dictated by his Platonism. Thus his stress on the total apathy of Christ, and on the ultimate putting off of that suffering flesh, is quite consistent with his view of man's nature and destiny. We might consider Clement, in that case, as one who developed a speculative theology on the basis of Middle Platonic ideas, and interpreted the biblical witness in those terms. This would be a modest thesis, in general acceptable to most scholars. But would it be the whole truth about Clement? I think it necessary to add at least the further thesis that at times Clement's philosophical ontology reduces Incarnation to charade, Christ's humanity to an unique occurrence robbed of genuine identification with "ordinary men," and the destiny of Christ--penetrating the noetic world apart from flesh because of his impassible soul--at odds with the biblical hope of resurrection.

(3) LIKENESS TO GOD

We shall endeavor, in a last systematic look at Clement, to indicate the main lines of his mystical theology. It is hoped that even a brief treatment of the subject will show its necessary place within the grand Alexandrian system of thought, and will suggest that it is indeed the key to it (QUASTEN: II.94ff; BOUYER: 256ff; DANIELOU 1948: 94ff, 1960: 217ff; VOLKER 1952). This is so even if Clement was not himself a "mystic." Charles Bigg's judgment is apt: "Clement shrank from his own conclusions. Though the father of all the Mystics he is no Mystic himself. He did not enter the 'enchanted garden' which he opened for others ... The instrument to which he looks for growth in knowledge is not trance, but the disciplined reason" (BIGG: 98).

'As Like God as Possible'

One of Clement's forceful illustrations describes the true believer or Christian gnostic: "Here it is we find the true wrestler, who in the amphitheatre of this fair universe is crowned for the true victory

over all his passions. For the president is God
Almighty, and the umpire is the only-begotten Son of
God, and the spectators are angels and gods, and our
great contest of all arms is not waged against flesh
and blood, but against the spiritual powers of passionate affections working in the flesh. When he has
come safe out of these mighty conflicts, and overthrown the tempter in the combats to which he has
challenged us, the Christian soldier wins immortality"
(*Str.* vii.III.20). His teaching on the Christian life
moves within two poles: man is made to become as like
God as possible; likeness to God consists in the habit
of impassibility.

The Platonists taught that the good life is
to be defined as eudaemonia, a process of "assimila-
ting the daemon more and more." After a Chapter on
opinions of various philosophers concerning the *summum
bonum*, Clement turns to Plato's opinion. "Now Plato
the philosopher, defining the goal of happiness
(*eudaimonian telos*), says that it is 'likeness to God
as far as possible'" (*Str.* ii.XIX.100.3). "Plato himself says that happiness is rightly to possess the
daemon, and that the soul's ruling faculty is called
daemon; and he terms happiness the most perfect and
complete good ... this he places in knowledge of the
Good, and in likeness to God, demonstrating likeness
to be justice and holiness with wisdom" (ii.XXII.131.4).
What sort of human life is agreeable to God? "That
which is characterized by one word of old: *Like will
be dear to like*, as to what is in proportion ... he
that would be dear to God, must, to the best of his
power, become such as He is. And in virtue of the
same reason, our temperate man (*sōphrōn*) is dear to
God. But he that has no self-control is unlike and
diverse" (132.4f). These last words are quoted from
the *Laws* (IV.716Cf); Clement now refers to the famous
saying of Socrates in *Theaetetus* 176B, "the way of
escape lies in becoming as like God as possible." Indeed, he quotes this twenty-two times in his writings
(STAHLIN (GCS) iv.50; MERKI: 44ff).

79

Two patterns are set before men, one divine and one godless, and "they are growing like the one and unlike the other ... they lead a life answering to the pattern which they resemble" (*Theaet.* 177A). Likeness to God may be understood, as Plato does in *Timaeus* 90D, as an imitation of the cosmic "harmonies and revolutions" discerned outwardly by astronomy and inwardly by intelligence. Or it may be understood with Aristotle in his final definition of human happiness or *eudaimonia* as an upward striving to approximate that which is "higher than the measure of humanity ... something within him that is divine" (*Eth. Nic.* 1177b 26ff). In either case it is a proportionate imitation of the measure provided by the divine life itself. Plato thought of the soul as *daimōn*, a kind of intermediary between man and God, in which the likeness or means to union is situated. Conformity to this inner principle brings conformity to God. Essentially, conformity means that self-control which patterns man's life after the peace and stability of the divine life. Likeness to God means impassibility. For "virtue" is not imitative but participative: the harmony of God himself shared by the rational soul.

Clement follows the formality of the philosophical teaching, but makes a decisive alteration by substituting "image" for daemon. The link is now the Logos, indeed the incarnate Word: "the image of God is the divine and royal Word, the impassible man; and the image of the image is the human mind" (*Str.* v.XIV. 94.5). The measure of likeness to God has been provided in Christ. "Grant to us who obey thy precepts, that we may perfect the likeness of the image" he prays (*Paed.* iii.XII.101.1). Christ declares, "I desire to restore you according to the archetype, that you may become also like me" (*Prot.* XII.120.4). Thus the Logos is both the image of God and the model after whom man is recreated: it is a fitting sequel to the Teacher's instruction by law and prophets, that he "should draw for us the model of the true life, and train humanity in Christ" (*Paed.* i.XII.98.1). The Christian is an image of the Image, a "third embodiment" of the divine likeness (cf *Paed.* i.XIII.101.2, for the Stoic formula (SC 70, 290)).

Man is a creature composed of body and mind,
two unequal parts that remind Clement of "the Centaur,
a Thessalian figment, compounded of a rational and irrational part, of soul and body" (*Str.* iv.III.9.4).
Yet the soul is not good by nature, nor the body bad:
superiority and inferiority are not so decisive as the
question of the "ruling spirit" which governs both (e.g.
iv.XXVI.164). The *hēgemonikon* as possibility derives
from man's *imago dei*; it becomes actual only as it
moves along the path of likeness. So the "image and
likeness of God" functions within Clement's anthropology
in a central manner. Like Philo, Clement found the term
homoiōsis in both *Genesis* 1:26 and *Theaetetus* 176B. He
relates them roughly as image to likeness, taking the
biblical "image" as applying to all men, whereas the
philosopher's "likeness" is a moral perfection to be
attained by the practice of virtue. It involves a distinctive *askēsis* of the Christian gnostic, a program
reminding us of Aristotle (LILLA: 106ff; FLOYD: 18ff).

Like Philo, Clement locates the divine image
in the rational soul, the human mind. Discussing the
various kinds of knowledge, for instance, he remarks
that in our capacity for gnosis, "knowledge of the
thing in itself ... the contemplation of realities,"
we resemble God, as well as in our having been made
immortal (*Str.* ii.XVII.76.3ff). There are three parts
to the soul (*Paed.* iii.I.1.2), intellect, emotion and
appetite; reason is always the governing principle or
the "pilot" (*hēgemonikos, kybernētēs*--e.g. *Str.* ii.XI.
51.6). This was the general Platonic approach, a
threefold partition of the soul, with three locations
in the body (head, heart, liver) and a corresponding
hierarchy of virtues (e.g. *Rep.* 443D.6f, *Tim.* 69Dff).
Philo had followed suit: "our soul is composed of
three parts, namely the rational, the irascible, and
the concupiscible (*logikon, thymikon, epithymētikon*).
We find that the seat and dwelling-place of the rational
part is the head, that of the irascible the breast, and
that of the concupiscible the abdomen" (*Leg. All.* 1.70f).

81

It is in this context that Clement refers to
the human *pathê*. "Appetite (*hormê*) therefore is a motion
of the mind to or from something. Passion (*pathos*) is
an excessive appetite beyond the bounds of reason, or
appetite unbridled and disobedient to reason. Passions,
then, are a perturbation (*kinêsis*) of the soul contrary
to nature, in disobedience of reason ..." (*Str.* ii.
XIII.59.6; cf iv.XXII.136.1, vi.XVI.135). Clement makes
the sharpest contrast between emotion and reason, the
irrational and the rational; thus the chief passions
such as *epithymia, hêdonê and orgê* "must have their
natural seat in the irrational part of the soul, also
be connected, in some way, both with sensation and with
body" (LILLA: 36). Yet we should note that certain
passions "exist for the maintenance of the body, such
as hunger, thirst and the like" (vi.IX.71.1). To these
even the gnostic is subject, since they are necessary
rather than wilful. He withdraws "his soul from passions" but not "himself from life" (75.3). It is the
second sort of passion, sufferings or the avoidable
motion of the soul, against which the gnostic has to
struggle. As we saw, Clement's christology is conditioned by this Platonic anthropology, for he maintains
that Christ had *neither* kind of passion.

Emotion, then, does not derive from reason
(e.g. by false judgment) but from bodily states and
seats. The "healing of our passions" comes from the
Logos, that Paedagogue who condescends to our weakness
and draws us gently toward the likeness of his own
passionless state (*Paed.* i.Iff; *Str.* iv.VI.40.1).

One passage, however, suggests a noteworthy
departure from this anthropology, and recalls Clement's
recognition of divine grace. "God has no natural
(*physikê*) relation to us, as the authors of the heresies will have it (neither on the supposition of his
having made us of nothing, nor on that of having formed
us from matter; because the former did not even exist,
while the latter is completely different from God) unless we shall dare to say that we are part of Him, and
of the same essence (*homoousious*) as God. And I do not

know how anyone who knows God can bear to hear this
when he looks at our life, and sees in what evils we
are involved ... But the mercy of God is rich toward
us, who are in no respect related to Him; I say
either in our essence or nature, or the peculiar
power of our being, but only in our being the work of
His will" (*Str*. ii.XVI.74^f; cf v.XIV.89.2f).

Beyond Faith: Knowledge

        The Word of God, for Clement, is explicitly
"intellectual" (*noeros*), and only in man is the image
of *mind* to be discovered. Therefore he can state that
"God is like man. For the distinctive form of each
one is the mind by which we are characterized" (*Str*.
vi.IX.72.2). Now mind is distinguished by its imper-
turbability, its freedom from the insecure motions of
the bodily. The pure mind, or Mind itself, will be
that which possesses an absolute immobility, the
singleness (*monadikos*) and composure of the contemplation of truth itself. Immutability and impassibility
are the crucial attributes of mind as it is distinguished from body in the Platonic universe. Clement
can proceed with logical precision, therefore, as he
describes the goal of the Christian Gnostic: "to become like his Teacher in impassibility" (*Str*. vi.IX.
72.1).

        The *homoiōsis* had been variously interpreted
by Middle Platonists such as Plutarch and Albinus, and
by Stoics and Neoplatonists. The former were content
to develop an ethic of moderation (*metriopatheia*),
while the latter pressed on to the full *apatheia*. We
saw above that Philo tended to accept the Aristotelian
mean of *eupatheia* for the majority of men, while re-
serving strict *apatheia* for the higher few such as
Moses, who attained "a complete absence of emotion"
(*Leg. All*. III.128). Where does Clement belong in
this scheme of ethics? Interpreters disagree as to
whether he is to be classified simply with Stoicism

or whether he modifies that position in a Christian direction (SPANNEUT: 231ff; VOLKER 1952: 507ff). The problem is probably solved by recognizing a two-step ethic in Clement, one preparatory and lower, in which moderate emotions such as kindness and steadfastness are directed toward helping the neighbour in imitation of Christ ("he who is made like the Saviour is devoted to saving," 77.5), and another both higher and enduring, in which every emotion is to be cut out (LILLA: 109ff; KIRK: 316ff; TOLLINTON 1914: II.90ff).

The true "likeness to God" is attained only at the higher stage, for the simplicity of deity is reflected only in man *monadikôs*. In describing the true gnostic in *Str.* iv, Clement quotes at one point the dictum of Pythagoras "Man ought to become one," and comments that God is one in the unalterable state (*ametatreptê hexis*) as creator of things good. Therefore when man becomes godly he becomes unified (*theoumenos, monadikos*: XXIII.151.3f). Now unity means harmony, the proportionate submission of all faculties under the government of reason. For both Pythagoras and Plato, such harmony is best cultivated through a curriculum involving those evident forms of proportionality: music, number, astronomy. Clement agrees, and devotes a chapter (XI) to the praise of mystical numerology, music (the Lord is Choir-master, directing those who "strike the chords of their souls" --88.3), and astronomy. After this curriculum (*encyclion*) philosophy supervenes, for "the mystery of truth" appears, the incarnate Word (95.1).

The Christian Gnostic ascends toward the goal of total *apatheia*, his desire set on it as the greatest good. Here is the perennial problem of mystical theology East and West, since *desire* is itself an affection indicating a need. Clement is well aware of the issue: "how, it is said, does he remain impassible who desires what is excellent?" And he provides an extensive answer. His chief point is that the nature of divine love is not properly "desire" (*epithymia*), nor does it constitute a need or lack

84

toward others, since he is entirely turned toward Christ
(vi.IX.71.4); it is an intentionality for whatever resembles excellence and goodness (*tois kalois kagathois*).
"And whoever is in the midst of that in which he is
destined to be, and has anticipated hope by knowledge,
does not desire anything, having, as far as possible,
the very thing desired" (73). The relationship of loving involves "affinity to the impassible God," a state
or habit in which there is "complete eradication of
desire." The fulfilment is explicit: "impassibility,
not moderation of passion" (*apatheia, metriopatheia,*
74.1). Being made perfect by love, the gnostic no
longer shares even in such rational affections as glad-
ness, dejection, caution and others which ordinarily
sustain the philosopher--they are now to him only
"petty and mean" compared with "the light inaccessible"
(75.1f; cf iii.VII.58: "we should do nothing from desire ... we are children not of desire but of will").

Clement's *gnôsis* represents a higher stage of
Christian perfection, beyond *pistis*. It reflects, in
part at least, the complex of ideas visible in the mysteries and esoteric gnosticism of the day, a fact over-
looked by Clement's apologists (e.g. GRILLMEIER,
CAMELOT; but see VOLKER 1952: 301ff; LILLA: 142ff).
The Christian is "destined to be divine ... already
being assimilated to God;" he "will one day become
god, aye and is even now being made like to God" (*Str.*
vii.I.3), indeed he "becomes a god while still moving
about in the flesh" (XVI.101.4). The succession to
gnosis is the fruit of mystic initiation, the aim of
askesis. In the final chapter of the "Exhortation"
(*Prot.* XII) Clement indulges in the rhetoric of
Christianity as the new and true mystery religion.
To the *mystês* he offers "initiation into the sacred
mysteries" and vision of those things "laid up in
heaven for me." "I will show you the Word, and the
mysteries of the Word." They are "dramas of the truth,"
"holy rites of the Word," "truly sacred mysteries."
Christ himself is "the hierophant" who illuminates the
initiate, introducing him to the Father, to survey
"the heavens and God." And he contrasts these

mysteries of the Logos with that "frantic intoxication" of the ecstatics: "I would invite him to the sobriety of salvation."

Now like Philo, Clement can distinguish *mikra mysteria* from *megala mysteria* (e.g. *Str*. i.I.15.3; iv.I.3.1; MARSH: 68f). But he does not intend by this distinction the progression, for example, from 'Exhortation' through 'Teaching' to ultimate secrets (cf LILLA: 190 correcting BIGG: 91). Rather, he takes the doctrine of creation as the lesser mystery from which one may proceed theologically to the greater. What is of more significance is the contrast between the apologetic mystery language of the *Protreptikos* and the developed teaching of an unwritten doctrine to be found throughout the Stromata. The latter restriction of truth to esoteric mystery suggests the need to speak of "two Clements, the Alexandrine philosopher and the Christian evangelist" (MARSH: 70). "And gnosis itself, having been imparted unwritten by the apostles, has descended by transmission to a few" (*Str*. vi.VII.61.3). The doctrine handed down *agraphôs* reflects his view of scripture as itself parabolic, a species of mystery cast in enigmatic utterances, thus testing the gnostic who is able to discern beyond the "secondary" a "primary" meaning (*Str*. vi.XV.126ff).

The gnostic passes beyond dependence on the written tradition and its witness to the historical Redeemer. His esoteric education shifts the focus to the Logos as Teacher, incarnate for a time in order to transmit the higher learning. The Stromata open with a clear enunciation of this doctrine. As a good Platonist Clement must comment on the wisdom of written documents. Writing is for the many; even Jesus spoke in parables, intimating that the ignorant crowd would not understand his teaching. There are two proclamations of the Word, one written and one oral, like the practice of the commandments or the partaking of the eucharist. So is the harvest twofold, unwritten and written. At this point Clement recounts his own pilgrimage from teacher to teacher, until in the last three (especially Pantaenus) he discovered those who preserved "the tradition of the blessed doctrine derived directly from the holy apostles, Peter, James, John and Paul" (*Str.* i.I.11.3).

The transmission to gnostic initiates of an esoteric *paradosis* is part of the Christian gnosticism which Clement develops. (There is also the philosophical tradition of unwritten "mysteries," e.g. *Theaet.* 156). It culminates, logically, in an immediate vision of God beyond the incarnate Logos parallel to the gnostic wisdom which he had appeared on earth to teach. Beyond the encyclical disciplines is the contemplation of transcendent reality; and beyond even that is the intellectual commerce with divine Being. The gnostic soul rises through the degrees of heavenly reality-- through seventh heaven to eighth (*Str.* vi.XIV.108.1)-- for it "presses on through the holy Hebdomad into the Father's house" (vii.X.57.5). A crucial chapter (*Str.* v.VI.32ff) provides an allegory of the Tabernacle, its furniture and High Priest. The interpretation draws heavily on Philo's *De Vita Mosis* book two (STAHLIN (GCS) ii.347ff), and its significance for Clement's gnosticism in relation to the *Himmelsreise* of the gnostic soul before and after death has been noted (MONDESERT: 172ff; LILLA: 173ff). Like the related passage of the *Exc. ex Theod.* 27, the High Priest's entry into the Holiest typifies the soul's entry into the heavenly realms. Man becomes *theophoros*, "controlled directly by the Lord and becoming, as it were, his body" (*Exc.* 27.6). The gnostic soul, purified of every passion and cleansed by the Word, ascends to "the ineffable inheritance of the spiritual and perfect man, 'which eye has not seen nor ear heard nor man's heart received,' and become son and friend, is filled with insatiable contemplation 'face to face'" (40.1).

The soul's rise to heavenly realms culminates in deification (*theopoieô*, *Protr.* XI.114.4). The gnostic's perfection, described at length in *Str.* vii, is that of becoming a spiritual temple, participating in the divine nature, "carrying God within him and being carried by God" (XI.64.7, I.3.1, XIII.82.2). Christ trains man "to adoption and salvation" in order to transform "earth-born man into a holy and heavenly being by His advent," communicating "the heavenly mode of life according to which we have been deified" (*Paed.* i.XII.98.3). Again, quoting Metrodorus the Epicurean (who spoke "divinely inspired"), concerning the soul's ascent to infinity, he continues, "when with the blessed choir, according to Plato, we shall gaze on the blessed vision, following with Zeus and others with other gods, if we may say so, to receive initiation into the most blessed mystery" (*Str.* v.XIV.138.3ff). Choosing the path of knowledge, the gnostic progresses into "the state of impassible identity" so that he no longer may be said to "have" but to *be* science and knowledge (*Str.* iv.VI.40.1).

Askêsis - the Gnostic Way

The brotherhood of philosophers in the classical world was characterized by a discipline of mind and body, a distinctive training, *askêsis*. Philo had used the term to describe the gymnastic of moral effort which is distinctive of those who practise wisdom; and the portrait of the ideal philosopher sketched by Epictetus illustrates it well. To live "in harmony with nature" requires progress in the discipline of self-knowledge: "to study to banish from one's life sorrows and lamentations and 'Alas!' and 'Wretched me!' and misfortune and failure--and to learn what death really is, and exile and imprisonment and the hemlock-draught, so as to be able to say in the prison, 'My dear Crito, if so it please the gods, so let it be.'" This is both Stoic and Cynic, both moral philosophy and theology, as Edwin Hatch maintained (HATCH: 139ff). By the second century A.D. the askesis had become regulated and familiar. The philosopher's gown, abstinence from wine, sleeping on the ground rather than a bed, the practice of "retreats," an occasional self-flagellation and binding--all these typify a philosophical monasticism that implies a religious cast to the doctrine of apathy or impassibility.

When Clement discourses on "the Lord's discipline" (*Str.* iv.VI.27.1) and describes its goal as "a passionless state ... a perfect man," we hear the theme of religious philosophy as it has been baptized into a doctrine of the Christian life. The gnostic undergoes an educative process by which the habit of Christ's *apatheia* is increasingly made his own. It is not a question of true humanity so much as of true divinity, which one receives through the illumination and discipline of the Word. Clement speaks of "the gnostic's apathy, if I may use the term, according to which the perfecting of the believer advances through love, till it arrives at the perfect man, at the measure of the stature, being made like to God and having become truly equal to the angels" (*Str.* vii.XIV.84). Gnosis provides a measure guiding us beyond the sense-world to the mind, a "decade" linked with the paschal feast of the tenth day, a transition "from objects of sense to those of the intellect," like the Passover transitus itself (ii.XI.50, 140).

The moral habit of apathy corresponds to the intellectual habit of "the apprehensive vision of the pure in heart." Union with Christ comes after cleansing by confession and vision by analysis (*Str.* v.XI.71). But although Clement can speak time and again of the gnostic's freedom from passion, "spotless purification" and attainment of the "summit" of contemplation, he speaks also of that which is the gnostic's "continual study and occupation," the service of God through liturgy, philanthropy and evangelism. Philip "killed his passions, and began to live unto Christ" (*Str.* iii.IV.25)—*apatheia* and *theōria* represent the ethical and theoretical aspects of *gnōsis* (LILLA: 163). The irrational emotions hinder the proper—"natural" and "rational"—life, namely contemplation, the goal of the wise man (vi.VII.61.2) and in itself "an eternal and immutable habit" (vi.VII.61.3, 69.1). If Clement accepts the formal analysis of Stoic ethics, he

89

recognizes that the positive virtues of the exemplar Christ provide a way out of the coldness of apathy (SPANNEUT: 231ff, 292f). Therefore his problematic, once again, is set by the philosophical *koinê* of the times, but this is threatened by the alien logic posed by an incarnational ethic of imitating a loving Saviour.

The divine is a model for human conduct, hence impassibility is Clement's ideal of human life. His critique of the Homeric pantheon rests on the negative of this principle: "Such gods let your boys be trained to worship, that they may grow up to be men with the accursed likeness of fornication on them received from the gods" (*Prot.* 2). False gods and demons are characterized by passion, but the true God is impassible. All this is clear, except that as we have seen, Clement does make place for the divine passion of love and its issue in the suffering of Christ. This is mirrored in the askesis of the Christian life. The gnostic must offer himself on behalf of the Church, he must stoop down from his impassibility "for the salvation of his neighbours" in imitation of the divine accommodation (*Str.* vii.IX.53).

In the present life, the Christian's service of God is the kindness and instruction by which he seeks to form others in the divine image (*Str.* vii. III.13; cf *Frag*, I, on I Pet. 2.9, STAHLIN (GCS) iii. 204, 21ff). The gnostic is a priest, is himself the altar as he offers the prayers which alone delight the God who needs nothing (*Str.* vii.VI.7). Thus the gnostic sacrifice mounts up as a "composite incense ... brought together in our songs of praise by purity and righteous and upright living grounded in holy actions and righteous prayer" (*Str.* vii.VI.33). Such a description of service can lead Clement to give explicit testimony to the ambiguity of the Christian's life--the true philosophy is both one and many, *both* apathy *and* "passionate desire" (*Str.* vi.VII.54.3). He can also express what will become a fruitful theme in subsequent theology of the spiritual life, that it

is *in via ad patriam*: "God has provided for us
another life and made the present life the way for the
course which leads to it; appointing the supplies derived from what we possess merely as provisions for
the way; and on our quitting this way, the wealth,
consisting of things which we possessed, journey no
farther with us" (*Frag.* II.1, V, *PG* 9.737--*Cat.* of
Nicetas on Job I.21).

The final note we should strike from the
wide range with which Clement supplies us, is one of
joy. This is a favorite theme in all his writings,
the peculiar delight of the Church, the new song of
praise which Christians have learned from the Word.
Cithaeron and Helicon are "now antiquated," the ancient
music and poetry, the Hellenic tragedy and mystery must
give place to "the new harmony which bears God's name
--the new, the Levitical song." In this whole passage,
at the beginning of the *Exhortation*, Clement gives the
closest scrutiny to the theme of "mystery and tragedy"
which we sketched in our opening chapter. He is pained
at the calamities that form the subjects of tragedy,
even though they are myths. For to make human woes
"the material of religious worship" is an invitation to
idolatry, so that "mysteries of deceit" arise. Men
are bound under the tyranny of demons in heathen worship, becoming monsters, beasts and stones. Then it
is that the Wisdom and Word of God appears, making men
out of stones and beasts, loosing them from demonic
bondage and raising them to contemplate heaven instead
of earth.

In such a vein Clement is the rhapsodist of
the new philosophy, the new mystery. For him the divine comedy has overcome the human tragedy. The
Christian's whole life has become a festival in which
he returns thanks "for knowledge bestowed and the gift
of heavenly citizenship" (*Str.* vii.VII.35, 49). Just
as the Word himself is "the New Song," so Christians
join in "the mystical chorus of the truth," for man
is created "a beautiful wind instrument of music."
The "mystic laughter" of Isaac (the meaning of the

Hebrew name was not missed by the Fathers) foreshadows
Christian joy, and in the Church men are called to
joyous service (e.g. *Prot.* I.6, XII.119). Perhaps this
climax to the *Paedagôgos* sums up his theme best (cf
BARDENHEWER: 57ff for the two hymns of the *Paed.*).
Like Anselm in a later age, he recognizes the connection between theology and doxology, and often forms his
theology as prayers offered to the God whom he seeks to
express. Therefore when he comes to the end of his
great discourse on the loving instruction of the Word,
he can but offer to Christ the Saviour "the reward of
due thanksgiving--praise suitable to his fair instruction." So grace begets gratitude:

> We, Christ-born, the choir of peace;
>   We, the people of his love,
> Let us sing, nor ever cease,
>   To the God of peace above.

CHAPTER 4

O R I G E N : T H E   M A S T E R

(1)   PRINCIPIA

"It was Origen's destiny to be a sign of
contradiction during his lifetime as well as after his
death" (QUASTEN: II.40). He would provide a bone of
contention in West as well as East, and remain even
today a suspect if not an outcast. Harnack believed
that he articulated a "Christian Hellenism" which was
to complicate the "inflexible Antignostic *regula
fidei*" (HARNACK 1961: II.12f). On this interpretation,
he courted the Gnostic "acute hellenization" of the
Gospel, despite his biblical norm and spiritual insight. Eugène de Faye promoted this critique, which
was given a better context by the research of Walther
Völker, Hal Koch and P.A. Lieske into Origen's mystical theology. Koch rejected Völker's positive assessment of Origen's doctrines of gnostic perfection and
mystical union (Logosmystik, Brautmystik, Gottesmystik
--VOLKER 1930: 98ff; KOCH: 329ff). Drawing a sharp
distinction between rational and mystical interpretations of Origen, he flung a challenge: "Between these
two conceptions must one choose; for my part I must
confess that the choice is not difficult" (KOCH: 342;
cf CROUZEL 1961: 530; HARL: 334f).

Our purpose here is to show how Origen develops the Philonic categories as filtered through
Clement's work, so that the problematics of approaching God "the anonymous" continued to shape the emerging
"classical theism" of the Church. We cannot accept
Koch's stark dichotomy. Origen does indeed resemble
Clement in the dominance of Platonism over his formulation of doctrine. Yet unlike Clement his mystical theology is more than an intellectual response
to a problem in epistemology. It functions as climax

and crucial step in the human pilgrimage of which he is truly a master of the spiritual life.

This remarkable Christian intellectual, who succeeded Clement as head of the catechetical school at eighteen years of age, defies simplistic assessment. He is rightly hailed as pioneer in the chief realms of Christian theology: biblical criticism and exegesis, systematics and apologetics. In approaching his doctrine of God, we must remember that "speculation" was proper and needful in an age of beginnings--apart from the question of the differing role of *theôria* in Eastern as against Western theology. Moreover, he is careful to distinguish between two areas of thought. The first is that in which he is reasoning within the common confession of faith, where "that alone is to be accepted as truth which differs in no respect from ecclesiastical and apostolical tradition" (*De Princ.* 2). The second is that in which doctrine is still "open," where he is relatively free to speculate, to suggest *gymnastikôs* theories about the origin of the soul, angelology, and especially cosmogony and eschatology. These latter two doctrines become at Origen's hands an eternal creation and the famous *apokatastasis* or restorationism which has characterized his name in popular opinion ever since.

'Illiberal Humanist'

Origen's is theology in grand scale. The reaches of his thought into the eternity before creation and after judgment suggest what is typical of the man, a *curiositas* wedded to an intense desire to glorify God by all human means, and in all human thought. Yet Origen is a child of his age, and his age was Platonist. As we have seen, its problems were expressed most clearly by the school of Middle Platonism. Origen's own methodology was patterned after this school's concern for *archai*, especially that ultimate Principle which is ineffable except through dialectical processes of abstraction or analogy. And his

94

great adversary Celsus who, though dead, spoke so
strongly that Origen was persuaded to answer him in
what is regarded as "the greatest apology of the primitive Church" (Quasten), belonged to this school.
Nor should we be surprised if Origen's answers to
Platonic questions are themselves--in form at least--
Platonic.

Origen presents a different attitude toward
philosophy from Clement. Whereas the latter was a
philosophical seeker and Christian convert, Origen's
parents were already Christian at least by the time
when their *Wunderkind* was ready for instruction, which
accordingly was strongly scriptural. The persecution
of 202/3 under Septimius Severus resulted in the death
of Origen's father Leonidas and the flight of Clement,
paving the way for the eighteen-year old to head the
"school." The young scholar exchanged his job as
teacher of grammar for that of catechist, rashly
selling "all his editions of the classics, beautiful
copies though they were" as Eusebius recounts. The
preparation for baptism in a time of persecution was
no mean task, and Origen determined to support his
vocation by a lifestyle which aimed at perfection--
what Eusebius called embarking on the "philosophers'
way of life." His extreme self-denial provoked gossip
about its source (so hard it is to believe in will-
power) and gave credence to the notorious story of his
self-castration. Henry Chadwick's comment is as far
as one should go: "told by Eusebius from hearsay and
possibly true" (CHADWICK 1967: 182; cf CHADWICK 1966:
67f; DANIELOU 1955: 12f). Such caution were better
than T.S. Eliot's image of "enervate Origen" whose
sterility reflects his "superfetation" of (or by) The
One (*Mr. Eliot's Sunday Morning Service*).

Launched on his new career, Origen soon
proved so successful that he gained an assistant to
take the initiates while he handled advanced studies.
Now began that life's work of erudite research which
puts him among the most formidable theologians of
history. He resumed his classical studies but in

strict relation to biblical exegesis, commentary and
speculation. We know of his method not only from his
own comments but particularly from his letter to his
pupil at Caesarea, Gregory Thaumaturgus, and Gregory's
famous panegyric to his teacher (about the year 238).
Origen now offers a course of study involving the
encyclia grammata which Clement had likewise endorsed
as preparation for Christian teaching. The crown of
this curriculum was philosophy. To Gregory he writes,
"I should like to see you use all the resources of your
mind on Christianity and make that your ultimate object.
I hope that to that end you will take from Greek philosophy everything capable of serving as an introduction
to Christianity and from geometry and astronomy all
ideas useful in expounding the Holy Scriptures; so that
what ... philosophers say of geometry, music, grammar,
rhetoric and astronomy--that they assist philosophy--
we too may be able to say of philosophy itself in relation to Christianity" (*Ep. Greg.* 1; DANIELOU 1955:
14ff). Origen proceeds to draw an analogy with the
Israelites' spoiling of the wealth of Egypt ("that is
to say, the world's knowledge"), although he warns of
the danger: "Having learned by experience, I assure
you that he is rare who takes the useful things of
Egypt, and comes out of it and fashions them for the
service of God, while Ader the Edomite has many a
brother. These are they who from some Greek liaison
beget heretical notions."

Origen has been styled "the illiberal humanist" (CHADWICK 1966: 66ff). The tension between
his classical humanism and his commitment to biblical
truth is indeed the key to the character of his work.
These two formative elements explain his stress on
divine *providence* and human *free will*. For instance,
to admit Gnostic doctrines would mean that "we should
no longer believe the world to have been made by God
nor to be ruled by his providence, and consequently
it would seem that no judgment of God on every man's
deeds is to be looked for" (*De Princ.* II.9.5).
Daniélou calls providence and merit his "two essential tenets" (DANIELOU 1955: 211). Origen accepts

the Homeric ideal of *aretê*, and the description of
human life as a ceaseless *agōn* against the passions.
Hence a moral ascent, a conscious striving, hones the
will and forms it to choose the good with increasing
power. But such stress on the will is subsumed under
a non-classical vision of the good: the process of
theōria, the development of human potential, is now
governed by the pedagogy of Logos. He it is who draws
the soul along the way of perfection, from the relative perfection of overcoming passion to the ultimate
perfection of God himself (JAEGER 1954: 86f; VOLKER
1930: 44ff).

Such an apologetic estimate of Origen reflects the modern judgment and breaks with traditional
condemnation. Eusebius had quoted Porphyry that
Origen "lived like a Christian, but on the realities
eternal and divine, he thought in Greek and brought
the hellenic concepts fraudulently under alien fables"
(*H.E.* VI.19.5ff). As Henri Crouzel warns, whoever
(like Harnack) seeks for "hellenism" in Origen will
surely find him "tout grec" but miss the essence
(CROUZEL 1962: 12). He is Greek in his concern for
the knowledge of God and for its necessary relationship to self-knowledge; but he denies the identification of the two kinds of knowledge, and wishes to let
the biblical Wisdom teach new data. He accuses Celsus
of suffering from "a vulgar and unphilosophical mind"
because he resorts to invective against Jesus rather
than to stating the facts and studying them "with an
open mind" (*C. Cels.* I.71). Indeed, "in philosophy
there are many charlatans" (*C. Cels.* IV.27). Like
Clement, he refers philosophy's truth to the general
beneficence of Wisdom, or to definitions (such as
"that the highest good is to become as far as possible like God") not discovered but lifted from scripture (e.g. *C. Cels.* VI.4, *De Princ.* VI.1.1). He
spends much time in refuting Celsus' charge that
Christianity demands obscurantism rather than
learning (*C. Cels.* III.44ff). In all this there is
expressed the patient and critical attitude of one
who committed himself to a life-long service of

scriptural study, served by all the humanistic or philosophical tools at his disposal. If his own form of "robbery" in despoiling this intellectual Egypt was often at graver risk than he imagined, nevertheless his vision and courage offer the only legitimate program for the theologian.

First Principles

A most thorough and profound critique of Christianity had been set forth by Celsus in his book *The True Word*. In one of its passages (all of which are available to us only because Origen's reply preserves them within his text) Celsus had declared that Plato is "a more effective teacher of the problems of theology." In support, Celsus quoted the familiar *Timaeus* passage about the difficulty of knowing God and the impossibility of declaring Him to all, with the comment: "You see how the way of truth is sought by seers and philosophers, and how Plato knew that it is impossible for all men to travel it. Since this is the reason why wise men have discovered it, that we might get some conception of the nameless First Being which manifests him either by synthesis with other things, or by analytical distinction from them, or by analogy, I would like to teach about that which is otherwise indescribable. But I would be amazed if you were able to follow, as you are completely bound to the flesh and see nothing pure " (*C. Cels.* VII.42). Thus the problem is clearly the knowledge of God or perhaps better, since "its context in the third century was mystical" as Daniélou reminds us, the problem of the *vision* of God (DANIELOU 1955: 104). The philosophical answer was that God is unknowable and nameless-- *arrêtos*. He can be known by abstraction and analogy. There is also involved the doctrine of the "second god," the Logos. Man attains the knowledge of God through the mediation of Logos and logoi, and not without the disciplined life of *apatheia* and the dialectic of analogical reasoning.

Origen is sympathetic to the Platonic answer.
He presupposes the theory of two contrasting worlds, one
intelligible and one sensible (e.g. *C. Cels.* VI.20,
VII.45f). He also presupposes such a degree of transcendence in God that He remains unknowable except to a
mind set free from the senses. This involves the doctrine that incorporeality is knowable only by similarly
incorporeal beings, and by the intellectual or spiritual faculty of man. Origen's systematic theology
defines God (*De Princ.* I.1.6) as follows: "God therefore must not be thought to be any kind of body, nor
to exist in a body, but to be a simple intellectual
existence, admitting in Himself of no addition whatever,
so that he cannot be believed to have in himself a more
or a less, but is Unity (*Monas*) or if I may so say,
Oneness (*Henas*) throughout, and the mind and fount
from which originates all intellectual existence or
mind." Again, against Celsus he writes, "Since we
affirm that the God of the universe is mind, or that
He transcends mind and being, and is simple and invisible and incorporeal, we would maintain that God is
not comprehended by any being other than that made in
the image of that mind" (VII.38). Here is the ontology
which determines both epistemology and soteriology:
God is of simple and intellectual nature, in a word
incorporeal, since matter is marked with mutability
and therefore with corruption. To be incorruptible
God must be unchangeable, and so immaterial. The chief
distinction between Creator and creation, indeed, is
that the latter is "of necessity subject to change and
alteration" (*De Princ.* II.9.2). This passage follows
Origen's declaration that in creating, God limited his
power since infinity defies understanding: "if the
divine power were infinite, of necessity it could not
even understand itself, since the infinite is by its
nature incomprehensible." His stress on providence is
his way of handling the thorny problem of the creative
action of infinite deity.

Can we *think* immaterial Being, infinite
deity? To describe God in terms of absolute simplicity and pure intellection would seem to remove that

which renders him knowable, except by a radical *via negationis* or learned ignorance. The Philonic categories reappear: God remains anonymous, incomprehensible in essence, without properties that might supply a name for human language. Origen, of course, has only begun; he proceeds to expound the way in which there is positive human knowledge of God. He shows that although God is incomprehensible there is no absolute darkness but a "véritable ésotérisme" of Light (VON BALTHASAR 1957: 33; cf HARL: 86ff for *dysgnôstos* as against *agnôstos*; FESTUGIERE: IV.92ff).

The precondition for knowing God is the fact that the human mind is itself an image of deity. Like knows like; mind comprehends Mind. The argument of Celsus which Origen seeks to refute in VII.32ff turns on whether the Christian doctrine of the resurrection is worthy of the invisible God or not. Origen agrees with Celsus' idealist presupposition, and states: "The knowledge of God is not derived from the eye of the body, but from the mind which sees that which is in the image of the Creator and by divine providence has received the power to know God" (VII.33). There is an intellectual sight which is different in kind from sensible sight: "in proportion to the degree in which the superior eye is awake and the sight of the senses is closed, the supreme God and His Son, who is the Logos and Wisdom and the other titles, are comprehended and seen by each man" (VII.39). To see the Word is to conceive the Father (*theôrein, katanoein*-- HARL: 188f).

Origen's doctrine of the revealing Logos is the dynamic of his epistemology: the various levels of being which participate in God begin with the Word (archetypal image) and move through "gods" (by participation of essence) to humanity (who can rise to participation through grace) (*In Joh.* II.32; cf I.268 - SC 120; *De Princ.* IV.4.5). The Logos--light of every being whether human or "powers" or angels-- condescends to assume such names as will lead men toward the proper and nameless One. Christ is the "express figure of the substance and subsistence of God" (*De Princ.* I.2.8), the "effulgence and image of the divine nature" (*C. Cels.* VII.17). God the Father alone is *autotheos* and "fountainhead of deity" (*pêgê tês theotêtos* - *In Joh.* II.2f); the Son is his eternal Wisdom: "the image of the unspeakable, unnameable, unutterable substance of the Father, his impress, the Word who knows the Father" (*De Princ.* IV.4.1). Though divine by right of eternal generation, the Logos can be defined by the problematic term "second god" (*deuteros theos* - *C. Cels.* V.39; *In Joh.* VI.39; *Dial. Herac.* 2). The Logos as archetypal image includes all *epinoiai*. Thus the Platonic quandary over mediation between the One and the many is solved by the Logos who is multiplex in his relatedness to worldly reality; indeed, original Wisdom is already manifold (*In Joh.* VII.7; cf I.157ff - SC 120.125ff, 212ff and 164f (note on *Theoi*); GRILLMEIER: 164ff).

The doctrine of the Son's eternal generation led Origen to coin the term *homoousios* to describe the "community of substance" between Father and Son (QUASTEN: II.78; KELLY: 130ff). Qualifying this point, however, is the notorious subordinationism of Origen's system. As second god, Logos is divine in a not quite identical mode of being, since he is image and agent of the Father. Prayer is not to be addressed to Christ, "but only to the God and Father of all, to whom also our Saviour prayed" (*De Orat.* 15.1). From the human point of view Christ appears equal with the Father; but within the triunity the Son conveys prayers to the Father, and with the Spirit is divine in a secondary way (cf OULTON-CHADWICK: 187ff, 346f). The subsequent debates of Origenism illustrate the master's difficulty in relating his transcendent Father to genuinely co-eternal Son and Spirit. In a functional sense, Logos appears similar to the first emanation of Gnostic schemes, or of the hierarchical speculation of Denis the Areopagite.

The problem resembles the Neoplatonic theology most of all. Plotinus' Nous was first emanation of the Abyss; Origen's Logos "had always gazed on the abyss of his Father's being" (*In Joh.* 2.2), and this creative contemplation is the source of his mediatorial office. He is both one and many. "The Father is purely and simply one, is absolutely simple, whereas there is multiplicity in our Saviour, because he was pre-ordained by God to make atonement for the whole of creation and be its first fruits: he was One, but for this reason he became Many as well" (*In Joh.* I.23). In His own being the Logos is the reconciliation of the One and the Many, of the transcendent being of the One and the multiple realm of inferior creatures: he echoes Clement's concept of the One as both One and One-Many. This ontological structure of mediation in terms of an idealist reconciliation of the one and the many is the possibility of atonement in the distinctively Christian sense. The question is whether his idealism--reflecting the "optimistic rationalism" of Greek philosophy--allows him to do justice to biblical history and eschatology. Thus he can state that the Logos is eternally Word, Wisdom, Truth and Life, and that he assumes new titles such as Redeemer and Shepherd; but the latter are temporal and ultimately accidental. One leaves them behind as he ascends through Christian gnosis to the reality of the eternal Logos, a process to concern us later. Here we must pursue the subject of the significance of the Logos and his soteriological properties.

Help from God

If God is unknowable He cannot be spoken of, and therefore man cannot give him a name. Such was the theology of the Platonists: for Albinus, God is transcendent so decisively that he is unspeakable and therefore unnameable (*arrêtos, akatonomastos*). Celsus had also stated that "he cannot be named" and Origen takes this up as worthy of a detailed reply. Celsus is right, Origen states, if he means that our descriptions by word or expression cannot show the divine attributes. But this applies to attribution on any level--"who can express in words the sweetness of a date and that of a dried fig?" There is difficulty in finding names to distinguish between qualities even in this regard (*C. Cels.* VI.65; cf VII.43--"we affirm that it is not only God who is nameless, but that there are also others among the beings inferior to him"). But if by "name" one means that he can "show something about His attributes in order to guide the hearer and to make him understand God's character insofar as some of His attributes are attainable by human nature," then this is a valid mode of speaking.

Origen is not suggesting that attribution is a logical process which provides a natural structure of ascending degrees to knowledge of God. He agrees with the assumption of Celsus that God "does not even participate in being," that He "has no experience which can be comprehended by a name," and is not "attainable by reason" (VI.64f). Rather, Origen's answer is in terms of the office of the Word. We shall illustrate this by considering a crucial passage, *C. Cels.* VII.42ff. The *Timaeus* statement of Plato, for instance, he admits as "noble and impressive." But does not God regard the needs of mankind better by the introduction of the divine Logos in the flesh? The incarnation of the Word renders Him "able to reach anybody." Here is where Origen's Platonism differs from the classical tradition in which Celsus and Clement stand: "Plato may say that it is difficult to find the maker and father of this universe, indicating that it is not impossible for human nature to find God in a degree worthy of Him, or if not worthy of Him, yet at least in a degree higher than that of the multitude ... we affirm that human nature is not sufficient in any way to seek for God and to find Him in His pure nature, unless it is helped by the God who is object of the search" (cf STANGE: 43ff).

Man knows God, Origen answers Celsus, "by looking at the image of the invisible God" (VII.43), that is "by a certain divine grace, which does not come about in the soul without God's action, but with a sort of inspiration" (VII.44). Plato had thought God difficult to know, but not impossible, whereas "it is probable that the knowledge of God is beyond the capacity of human nature (that is why there are such great errors about God among men), but that by God's kindness and love to man and by a miraculous divine grace the knowledge of God extends to those who by God's foreknowledge have been previously determined, because they would live lives worthy of Him after He was made known to them" (VII.44). The problem raised by the idea of divine predestination as foreknowledge need not detain us; the point is Origen's rejection of the Platonic trust in a natural capacity to know God. In the Celsus argument he is refuting we have a clear expression of the *triplex via* already examined in Albinus and Clement. Celsus had stated that wise men had discovered "the way of truth," in order that "we might get some conception of the nameless First Being which manifests him either by synthesis with other things, or by analytical distinction from them, or by analogy" (VII.42). It is to this self-confidence of the philosophical ways that Origen recommends the humbler way of divine grace. One cannot reach "the threshold of the Good" by any means other than "a certain divine grace ... a sort of inspiration" (VII.44).

Jean Daniélou's reading of these critical sections holds that Origen shares Celsus' opinion as to the intrinsic validity of the methods of abstraction and analogy; he concludes, "Celsus had agreed with Plato that the vision of God is within man's reach but at the price of great effort, and that it is the privilege of the few. Origen rejects both propositions" (DANIELOU 1955: 107). It seems that however seriously Origen takes the philosophical reasoning involved in meditating on the data of faith, unlike Clement he posits an analogy of grace at the heart of man's knowledge of God. This same analogy may count against de Faye's estimate: "The God he conceives is more abstract than the God of Plato himself" (DE FAYE 1926: 55). Despite the attraction of his Platonic milieu, despite his commitment to its epistemology of the two realms, he cannot be relegated simply to the polarities of its logic.

It is likely that he heard the lectures of Ammonius Saccas, founder of Neoplatonism, and his ideas make contact with those of Plotinus at certain points. Daniélou holds that Origen probably was not a pupil of Saccas, nor acquainted with Plotinus, their affinity being accounted for in terms of their "common set of problems" and the "common influences" of the day (DANIELOU 1955: 76ff). Chadwick, however, writes: "For a time he studied Greek philosophy in the lecture room of Ammonius Saccas, with whom Plotinus was later to study for eleven years" (CHADWICK 1967: 182). Regardless of this debate, it is clear that he pursued his ideas in light of a quite different datum peculiar to his Christian tradition, the incarnation of the Word. For, "the aid of the author and creator himself was demanded" (*De Princ.* III.5.6).

Origen casts his thought in forms given by the Greek philosophical *koinê* already noted. But insofar as his train of thought is itself powered by an alien datum, there results a tension and an ambiguity, the mixed heritage our thesis proposes. There is strength to the summary of Hal Koch, that Origen's theology involves a meeting of divine providence and human learning: *pronoia* and *paideusis*. The education of humanity takes place through the providential teaching of the Incarnate Word: Logos is Paidagogos (KOCH: 3, 62ff). Origen at the last has to grapple with the logic of this dynamic role for Logos: how can such lively *paideia* spring from the changeless One?

Origen's theology is in praise of divine
glory--the utter transcendence of God, "far removed
from every feeling of passion or change" (*ab omni
passionis et permutationis effectu--Hom. Num.* 23.2 -
PL 12, 748; SC 29, 439). He must grapple with the
question raised by such radical transcendentalism,
therefore: can God be not only transcendent and
abstract but also "le Vivant par excellence?"
(DE FAYE 1925: 49). Harnack was convinced that
"Origen raised the thought of the unchangeableness
of God to be the norm of his system" (HARNACK 1961:
II.342). Over against such interpreters as Harnack,
De Faye and Hal Koch, however, are those who see
Origen's liaison with Hellenism as less than decisive,
since his biblical orientation was powerful enough to
guide him through the dialectic of transcendence and
immanence without ultimate harm (CROUZEL 1962: 11ff;
DANIELOU 1955: xvi). The question has never been
merely academic. In Origen's time not only Gnostic
and Manichaean but also Stoic had to admit some degree
of mutability in God as they struggled with the problem of the relationship of divinity to matter.
Aristotle's transcendent deity had not solved the
problem, even for the philosopher himself. God was
pure spirit, or pure spirituality, and yet he "acted"
upon matter, as the unmoved mover (*Meta.* 258bf;
Phys. viii; cf JAEGER 1934: 342ff). For Origen, the
question is approached in terms of the Platonic doctrine of model and image, and of the place of the
Incarnate Word in this kind of universe. He faces
a profound difficulty in all this, because he is opposing those (Stoics, Epicurus, even Aristotle) who
have filled the world "with a doctrine that abolishes
providence, or limits it, or introduces a corruptible
first principle which is corporeal," while "the
doctrine of the Jews and Christians which preserves
the unchangeable and unalterable nature of God has

been regarded as irreverent, since it is not in agreement with those who hold impious opinions about God"
(*C. Cels.* I.21).

Analogy and Incarnation

It is a firm belief of Origen's that there
is a law of correspondence between the heavenly and
the earthly realms of being. Like Clement he accepts
the Platonic *chōrismos* between sensible and intelligible realms. He takes it further in his anthropology:
man is microcosm of the macrocosm; and gives the whole
concept of correspondence a scriptural basis. In expounding the Song of Songs, Origen collates passages
about animals in order to group together the visible
or manifest things so that he may learn from them
things invisible and hidden, for "all things visible
have some invisible likeness and pattern" (*In Cant.*
III.12). It is because "this earthly scene contains
patterns of things heavenly" that one can mount up
from the one to the other. Indeed, he continues,
"perhaps the correspondence between all things on
earth and their celestial prototypes goes so far"
that even vegetable life participates in it. Not only
has man an image and likeness of divinity, but animal
and vegetable life also exhibit the pattern of the
kingdom of heaven.

Origen's method of allegorical interpretation reflects this Platonic theory of correspondence,
of image and reality. There is a realm of historical
images, a Church and a Gospel for instance, and there
is a higher realm of heavenly realities, a "Spiritual
Church" and an "Eternal Gospel." The significance of
this theory for the Incarnation is crucial. The
Christ of history is the temporal and temporary manifestation of the eternal Word, destined to be transcended as the Christian gnostic attains the higher
truth of such manifestations. The Logos reveals
himself through a series of *epinoiai*, whose lower

107

forms, such as redemption and mediation, serve for
human needs in the present world but will be super-
seded in the aeons to come. All this is especially
clear in Origen's commentary on the Gospel of John.

There was a Gospel in the Old Testament, for
the Word was known spiritually by certain saints who
saw through "the veil which was present in the law and
the prophets," the types and shadows of the old
covenant (*In Joh*. I.8). Such a person knew that God
is a spirit, and worshipped Him spiritually, "no
longer by type does he worship the Father and Maker
of all." In St. John's Gospel we see most clearly
the distinction between somatic and spiritual forms
of the Gospel. The spiritual or eternal Gospel leads
into "the mysteries presented by His discourses and
those matters of which His acts were the enigmas"
(I.9). There is a distinction between two kinds of
Christian, therefore--but out of love to men, the
spiritual Christian continues to speak as a somatic
one, "where there is a call for the bodily Gospel, in
which a man says to those who are carnal that he knows
nothing but Jesus Christ and Him crucified."

Origen's aim is to develop the spiritual
Gospel from the bodily one. "What we have now to do
is to transform the sensible Gospel into a spiritual
one ... our whole energy is now to be directed to the
effort to penetrate to the deep things of the meaning
of the Gospel and to search out the truth that is in
it when divested of types" (I.10). Now I submit that
this method of Origen's is not a problem in the relationship between the historical records and
Christian faith as Henri de Lubac suggests, but is
the more serious problem of history itself (DE LUBAC
1950: 92ff). It is true that Origen seeks to show
his regard for the historical nature of the Biblical
narrative. In the famous passage where he states
that "occasionally the records taken in a literal
sense are not true, but actually absurd and impossible"
(*De Princ*. IV.3.4), he goes on to emphasize the basic
historicity of Scripture. Lest he be suspected of

saying that none of the history happened, or that no
law is to be kept literally, or "that the records of
the Saviour's life are not true in a physical sense,"
he insists "that in regard to some things we are
clearly aware that the historical fact is true ...
For the passages which are historically true are far
more numerous than those which are composed with
purely spiritual meanings." Yet Origen's insistence
does not touch his basic assumption that history itself is but an image of eternity, so that his defense
of the historical remains ambiguous.

When Origen states that certain things actually happened in the life of Christ, he means that
they happened on the plane of history and therefore
constitute *typoi*. Now "types" for him are by definition temporal and temporary. "For we ought not to
suppose that historical things are types of historical
things, and material things of material, but that
material things are typical of spiritual things, and
historical things of intellectual" (*In Joh.* X.14).
When such typological theory is applied to the concept
of the incarnation of the Word, there seems to be
finally a denial of ultimate or decisive significance.
On this point of controversy in the interpretation of
Origen, the work of M. Harl argues strongly that the
orientation toward the historical Jesus is soon displaced by the conceptuality of a dual Christ, temporal
and eternal (HARL: 121ff; but cf DE LUBAC 1950: 219ff;
CROUZEL 1961: 324ff). That is, whatever typology of
the horizontal thrust of history presents itself is
set against an overpowering "vertical" symbolism of
two realms. Jesus is historical "shadow" and "image"
of the eternal Word, and there remains a final ambiguity to the Word incarnate (HARL: 139ff, 191ff).
Origen's vision of the eternal and transcendent One
so impressed him with attributes of eternity and
transcendence that he could not conceive of history
and immanence as providing attributes of equal status.
If Logos assumed humanity, this could not be other
than a temporary accommodation until the cure was
effected and the pure intellect enabled to ascend to

an eternal vision of the eternal One. This transcendentalism of both ontology and epistemology, therefore,
provides sufficient explanation for Origen's hesitation
in his treatment of the role of incarnation. And it
leads into the complex and deepest problems of philosophy and theology: the very nature of God and man and
the question whether the Christian doctrine of the
Trinity is a necessary and a sufficient articulation
of truth.

It is when Origen handles the titles of
Christ that he formulates his own answer. His introduction to the commentary on John is a treatise on the
epinoiai. The manifold functions of the Logos are expressed through his titles: word, wisdom, redeemer,
shepherd, etc. It would seem that "Word" is the
highest, the eternal title, and yet: "if we go
through all his titles carefully we find that he is
the *archê* only in respect of his being wisdom. Not
even as the Word is he the *archê*, for the Word was in
the *archê*. And so one might venture to say that
wisdom is anterior to all the thoughts that are expressed in the titles of this first-born of every
creature" (I.22). This does not mean, however, that
the title of Word is not crucial, since it is *Logos*
which on investigation forces theology to reckon with
positing a second, "separate entity," a Son of God,
and so to examine all other titles (I.23).

In acknowledging Wisdom as the only attribute properly eternal, a distinct problem is posed
by the text of *I Cor*. 1:30: "Christ Jesus, whom
God made our wisdom, our righteousness and sanctification and redemption." For once having settled the
question of an "eternal" or absolute title, Origen
wishes to show that all other titles were taken by
Wisdom "for us," in accommodation to human needs
rather than in expression of divine verities. He
explains Paul's words by referring them to other
passages which call the Son wisdom (and "power") in
an absolute sense (I.39). Thus we have "both forms
of the statement, the relative and the absolute"

whereas with the other titles such as sanctification and redemption we have only the relative. Origen's purpose is to distinguish the higher titles, including Wisdom, Word, Life and Truth from those which are later, "which he took for our sake." Divine providence has met human need and human potential by supplying the variety of titles to lead us along the way of attribution toward the absolute and ultimate *Archê*. And a crucial passage observes, "happy indeed are those who in their need for the Son of God have yet become such persons as not to need him in his character as a physician healing the sick, nor in that of a shepherd, nor in that of redemption, but only in his characters as wisdom, as the word and righteousness, or if there be any other title suitable for those who are so perfect as to receive him in his fairest characters" (I.22).

The distinction between simpler and higher believers has returned, as it must once we accept a distinction between realms of being. We saw that Clement (and Philo) considered it necessary to assign a difference in kind between the two. Harry Wolfson's thesis is that while Origen agrees that there is "a great difference between knowledge conjoined with faith and faith only," he yet holds to the "single faith" theory as against Clement's "double faith" (WOLFSON 1956: 106, 120; BARDY: 1514ff). If we view Origen's theology of the spiritual life and the mystical-eschatological element, we may agree that he holds a single faith theory, reducing differences among believers to stages on the way of Life. Yet in view of his more philosophical speculation on *Theos-Theoi* and *Logos-Logoi*, it seems that the ambiguity remains here too. For he can state clearly that the "class" of believer that holds to Reason is quite distinct from that whose members "know nothing but Jesus Christ and him crucified, considering that the Word made flesh is the whole Word, and knowing only Christ after the flesh. Such is the great multitude of those who are counted believers." The two classes have "analogies in what concerns the Logos. Some are

adorned with the Word himself; some with what is next
to him but appears to be the very original Logos himself, those, namely, who know nothing but Jesus Christ
and him crucified, and who behold the Word as flesh"
(II.3). The Logos "is not on earth as he is in
heaven; on earth he is made flesh and speaks through
shadow, type and image." Origen concludes: "The
multitude, therefore, of those who are reputed to believe are disciples of the shadow of the Word, not of
the true Word of God which is in the opened heaven"
(II.4).

Now some kind of progression in man's reception of the Word is to be expected. There is milk
and there is meat, and a growth is discernible in
those who develop from the one to the other (e.g.
I. Cor. 3, *Gal.* 3:12ff, *Heb.* 5:11ff). Origen has a
full discussion of this subject in his comments on the
petition "Give us this day our daily bread" (*De Orat.*
27). The Word is milk for those Christians who are
like children, vegetables for those who are weak, and
solid meat "adapted to athletes" for those engaged in
active combat (para. 9). The solid form of the
"living bread" is "spiritual and reasonable food"
shared with angels, and confers deification. Origen's
argument turns on (what he takes as) the root *ousia* in
the phrase "daily (*epiousios*) bread." The particular
"substance" of the living bread apprehended by the
spiritual and reasonable gnostic Christian is the incorporeal substance of divinity: "epiousios bread is
that which is best adapted to the reasonable nature
and akin to it in its very substance: it provides at
once health and vigor and strength to the soul and
imparts a share of its own immortality (for the word
of God is immortal) to him who eats of it" (JAY: 220ff
(App. F); CROUZEL 1962: 21).

Origen's conception of the offices of Christ
assumed in incarnation depends on prior questions of
the relative significance of history and the dual
nature of man. The "spiritual and reasonable" in man
is his higher nature, capable of apprehending divine

reality and of deification. This requires a discipline
of the body and an ascent of the soul on the part of
the gnostic, as we shall see in the next section. Our
point here is that the formal steps of this ascent are
provided by God in the descent of Logos through a number of lower forms, adapted to the varying capacities
of men. Thus the natural analogy of history and eternity, of earth and heaven, of letter and spirit, is
subsumed under the incarnation of the Word. But by
the same token, the incarnate Word participates in the
relative and temporary nature of the world into which
he comes. The truth of Gospel consists in apprehending a gracious divine-human reality, to be sure, but
there follows recognition of the merely symbolic nature
of the human element and ascension to the divine reality
above it.

Thus Origen is committed to the incarnation
as the decisive Christian dogma; yet his Platonism
provides the horizon against which the historical
Jesus is but occasion for the Christian's ascent to
full participation in divine being. "When all is said
and done Christ is in danger of being still only a
'quantitatively' different exceptional case of the
universal relationship of the 'perfect' to the Logos"
(GRILLMEIER: 169). The question at issue here is not
solved by supposing an Alexandrian "allegorical" as
against an Antiochene "literal" interpretation of
Scripture. As Daniélou has demonstrated, "The
exegesis of both was typological and the one was as
Christological as the other" (DANIELOU 1955: 164).
In the Hellenistic world, *historia* signified that re-
porting of worldly events which Plato relegated to
mere *mythos* as compared with the genuine *logos* involved
in understanding the world of intelligibles. Justin
had denoted the literal sense of the Mosaic writings
as *historia*, and Antioch agreed. Origen's predilection
for the Platonic *chōrismos* steered him away from that
option so that he served to widen "even further the
gulf separating the methods and matter of *historia*
from the study of the true actions of God in behalf of

his creatures" (PATTERSON: 55). The fateful philosophical dichotomy continued to have theological consequences, especially in that crucial topic, the
meaning of history.

Light Into Love: Accommodation

        The logic of Christian Hellenism involves
that theological model we are denoting by the phrase
"God the anonymous." This model presses an extreme
use of the negative mode--in divine attribution and
therefore proportionately in both religious language
and spirituality. A sort of methodological *askēsis*
obtains, a severe qualification to every positive
modality of human thought, language and action. If
this were the whole story, the Alexandrians would have
been guilty of a species of *re*-mythologization, taking
Platonism as normative and fitting Christianity into
the developed scheme we have examined. Because this
is not the whole story, because Clement and Origen
committed themselves to their scriptural material,
therefore a mixed blessing results. In this mixture
there is faith and also knowledge, and "faith" *tends*
to play the role which *doxa,* opinion, held in Plato's
epistemology. We saw how Clement's gnosticism pre-
vented his adequate articulation of the incarnation,
since his faithfulness to concepts of immutability
and impassibility governed his christology. In
Origen's case a similar impasse results in most of
his work, despite his greatness as biblical exegete
and preacher. This is so because he is fitting
Scripture into a grand design patterned after Platonic
and Stoic models of heavenly realms and successive
aeons, a systematization which links him "with
Valentinus, his forerunner, and Plotinus, his successor" (DANIELOU-MARROU: 185).

        Origen's vision of pre-existent spirits
fallen into historical being and rescued by divine
pedagogy takes the biblical material seriously, but

114

only up to a point, or rather within two points. It
is a kind of parenthesis, a happening valid as cure,
as means to a higher end. The story of redemption
is a lower truth, very similar to Plato's definition
of myth as "likely story," and fulfilling a similar
function. The *higher* truth, logos rather than mythos,
is reserved for those who see through the veil and
recognize its nature as both temporary and temporal.
It is this schematization of Origen's which leads
R.P.C. Hanson to describe the "spiritual Gospel" as
"not a Platonized form of genuine Christian eschatology, but an alternative to eschatology, indeed an
evasion of it," and Daniélou to agree with von Ivanka
that "it introduced the facts of Christianity into a
framework whereby restoration to the pristine state
renders void its real historicity, the decisive
characteristic of Christianity, and ends by diluting
Christ's action into a kind of cosmic process"
(HANSON 1959: 354; DANIELOU-MARROU: 186).

Origen's analytic of the biblical history
and imagery, we might say, is ultimately compromised
by the "synthetic *a priori*" according to which he defines and polarizes both history and imagery as such.
His method of interpretation is perhaps improperly
named "allegorical," if we attend to those scholars
who clarify the differences among the typology of
Justin, Melito and Irenaeus, the allegory of Clement,
and Origen's mixed exegesis. Sometimes he draws on
both those traditions, but he also introduces another
kind of allegory, not arguing from a historical
"sense" to an allegorical, but relegating the entire
biblical witness to "an immense allegory" (DANIELOU-
MARROU: 186). This does not deny the historicity--
it is not the sort of allegory for which moral fables
would serve as well; rather it is closer to what is
intended by the term *anagōgē*. The latter would become a technical term for an Origenist such as
Didymus the Blind (BIENERT: 32ff, 63ff), and designate
the final sense in the fourfold exegesis of medieval
scholarship. For Origen, the anagogical sense is
that mystical way from letter to spirit, from earthly
and historical image to heavenly and eternal truth.

Henri de Lubac puts it: "L'esprit ne se découvre
que par *anagogie* ... Il nous faut par consequent
toujours *anagein tēn historian*" (DE LUBAC 1950: 284;
cf 304ff). The question is not whether such distinctions are in order—one thinks of the famous threefold
scheme of Ambrose: *umbra, imago, veritas*—but whether
they represent an ultimate dichotomy in which the
biblical witness is but foil to a supreme and gnostic
allegory. In this regard one might indeed speak of
"enervate Origen."

Anagogy suggests the gnostic perspective.
The Old Testament events, for instance, no longer pre-
figure the coming Jerusalem; rather, "he reverses the
order and looks on them as an image of the past history of a higher world ... That shows the subversive
influence of the gnostic outlook both on Origen's
exegesis and on his theology" (DANIELOU 1955: 196).
There is indeed a case of model and image, or archetype and ectype, corresponding to the modern "promise
and fulfilment" for example; and Origen contributes
greatly to our appreciation of the biblical story
and its development or economy. Yet he insists that
all this is part of the less important story condemned
by its historicity to but passing honor. The irony is
that this vision which gives his biblical homilies
such power for spirituality makes them questionable
aids for theology. Therefore this irony must question
that spirituality itself—does knowledge of the
anonymous God require such mystical anonymity of the
human knower that he ceases to be defined with reference to the biblical events at all?

Origen is a leading creditor of historical
theology through his fine exposition of such concepts
as providence and accommodation (HANSON 1959: 210ff;
DREWERY: 86ff, 103ff). Later trinitarian debates
explore choices such as "essential" and "economic" or
modes of "being" as against modes of "revelation;" for
Origen the choice was rather between God as Light and
as Love. It seems proper to define the utterly transcendent One as Light: He *is*; therefore all others are,

116

and can see what is. Now even light is analogue, but its claim to priority consists in the grandeur of its essential remoteness, the tranquillity of its static perfection. To turn from that to the attribute of love, to say that God is Love, is to enter an alien realm of dynamism and the motions of grace and faith-- and perhaps their opposites. Although it may be true that "Origen's thought leads to a real philosophy of history, a thing that never grew on the soil of classical Greece" (JAEGER 1961: 63), this philosophy at last treats history as less than true, and other than decisive. Origen remains faithful to the opposing realms of Hellenism, or indeed to the subtler refinement of "three cities"--natural, spiritual and intellectual, with the last, the intelligible world, beyond grace itself (CADIOU 1935: 281ff).

The question of the divine *descent* in incarnation is therefore decisive for the entire theology of Origen. Celsus had brought the objection "that we affirm that *God Himself will come down to men*. And he thinks it follows from this that *He leaves his throne*" (*C. Cels.* IV.5). But Celsus, replies Origen, does not know the power of God, for He both fills all things and maintains all things in their being. If God is said to descend, or if the Word "comes to us," this does not mean that He moves from one place to another or leaves his throne. There is no "changing" or "leaving" involved (cf VI.60ff). "Even supposing that we do say that He leaves one place and fills another, we would not mean this in a spatial sense." In what sense would we mean it? In an existential sense, for the "change" is to be understood as taking place *in us*: "anyone who has received the coming of the Word of God into his own soul changes from bad to good, from licentiousness to self-control, and from superstition to piety." One scholar has concluded that for Origen, "The earthly life of Christ was a grand symbolic drama, a divine mystery-play for the enlightenment of humanity" (INGE: 9).

Origen makes excellent use of the category of *condescension* to illustrate the divine *katabasis*. When the prophets speak of a divine descent, this is symbolic and refers to God's coming down from majesty to care for human affairs. "Just as people commonly say that teachers come down to the level of children, and wise men or advanced students to those only recently led to study philosophy, without meaning that they make a physical descent; so, if anywhere in the divine scriptures God is said to 'come down,' it is to be understood in a similar sense to that of the common usage" (*C. Cels.* IV.12). A striking passage in a homily on Jeremiah expresses the Alexandrian *paideia:* "Picking them out, you might discover a thousand other passages from the holy Scriptures, with which to class the saying, God is not as man. But when the divine activity is concerned with the affairs of men, then it takes on the mind of a man, his character, his ways of speech. In like manner, if we are talking to a child of two years old, we use baby language for the child's sake. For it is impossible if we preserve the style appropriate to the age of a full-grown man and speak to children without any condescension to their way of talking, for children to understand. Conceive, I pray you, something of this sort in regard to God in his dealings with the race of men ..." (*Hom. Jerem.* xviii.6 cf *C. Cels.* IV.71 on "talking with little children.") A striking parallel (or borrowing?) is offered by Calvin's comment on John 3:12: "God comes down to *earth* that He may raise us up to *heaven* ... He condescends to our ignorance. Therefore when God prattles (*balbutit*) to us in Scripture in a rough and ready style, let us know that this is done on account of the love He bears to us" (*Comm. ad loc.*).

The problem of Celsus' appears most important to Origen, and he returns to it a second time (IV.14ff). Since God is "good and beautiful and happy, and exists in the most beautiful state" as Celsus puts it, how can he be spoken of as changing? Only the nature of a mortal being suffers change. Origen refers to his former reply, and adds, "While remaining unchanged in

118

essence, He comes down in His providence and care over human affairs." He distinguishes this doctrine from that of Epicurus and the Stoics, for they have missed "the true conception of God's nature, as being entirely incorruptible, simple, uncompounded, and indivisible." So also (IV.15), Christ was in the form of God but emptied Himself, that men might be able to receive Him. "But He underwent no change from good to bad." When the Word assumed a human body and a human soul, He remained "Word in essence," suffering "nothing of the experience of the body or the soul." His descent is to the low level of those who cannot behold the divine radiance; He "becomes as it were flesh, and is spoken of in physical terms, until he who has accepted him in this form is gradually lifted up by the Word and can look even upon, so to speak, his absolute form."

Here is where his doctrine of the *forms* of the Word receives full weight (DREWERY: 115ff). There are different forms corresponding to the different kinds of receivers—"whether he is a beginner, or has made a little progress, or is considerably advanced, or has nearly attained to virtue already, or has in fact attained it" (IV.16). A favorite illustration in this respect is the Transfiguration story (e.g. II.64). The people down below could not receive the truer form in which he showed himself to the chosen few on the mountain. The former saw only the mortal nature (Origen quotes Isaiah 53, "he had no form or beauty"), while the disciples attained to the immortal Logos. Yet Origen does not wish to suggest that the human form is an appearance only—"he does not mislead or tell lies" (IV.18). Although he will not say that the incarnate form partakes of an absolute character, he is not saying the opposite, in the Gnostic manner of reducing the incarnation to an appearance of relative value—a sort of theophany. He wishes to maintain its truth as preparatory rather than normative. Again it is pedagogy which is operative: the divine Logos assumes humanity in relation to our present fallen state, for we "could only thus at first receive him" (*In Joh.* I.20). Even though Christ's death will hold for all aeons, it is its eternal truth which avails (*In Rom.* 5.10).

It is for such reasons that Kelly states, "It must be recognized that the incarnation as such really stood outside the logic of Origen's system ... The mediator between the only true God, i.e. the ineffable Father, and man is not, in the last analysis, the God-man Jesus Christ, but the Word Who bridges the gulf between the unoriginate Godhead and creatures" (KELLY: 157). This suggests why Origen's insistence against Celsus that Logos assumed a true human soul and body passes into the view that both soul and body are changed by the union "in a superior and more divine way" (II.9). Referring to the philosophical theory that bodies receive various qualities, he can affirm that the body of Jesus was obviously patient of "ethereal and divine quality" (III.41). Anticipating such eschatological transformation is his ability, as noted in regard to the Transfiguration, to change appearance--not only as to his divinity "but also as to his body which was transfigured when he wished and before whom he wished" (II.64).

So Origen's philosophy of history--more properly, "philosophy of aeons"--entails a view of incarnation as temporary and relative, an earthly manifestation of higher principle and being, apparently as close to Docetism as was Clement's christology. Incarnation is interlude: commenting on John 10:8, he suggests that after the consummation "he may be such as he was before he emptied himself" so that it will be the Father alone who says, "Behold, I am with you." On such a view we would expect the question of impassibility to provide a touchstone to judge this dilemma of "changeless yet lively."

The Suffering of Christ's Soul

A distinctive feature of Origen's christology is his concept of Christ's *human soul*. It is related to the Platonic doctrine of the pre-existence of souls and the Stoic doctrine of hegemony. Origen's anthro-

pology posits three elements, body, unreasoning soul
and reasoning soul. The last is properly called
"spirit" and is pre-existent and unchanging, like God.
His doctrine of pre-existence, the subject of the
Anathemas of Second Constantinople, 553 (*De Princ.*
II.8.3 - Butterworth ed. 125f; MANSI: IX.395ff)
supposed an original creation in which "all rational
creatures" existed in unity by participation in the
"divine love and contemplation." Weariness with this
state caused their fall into union with bodies of
various degrees and names (in the blessed state they
had been anonymous). This ontological presupposition
informs Origen's doctrine of the Incarnation (*De
Princ.* II.6), at which he marvels in expressions of
astonishment. The key concept is the human soul of
Jesus. "This soul, then, acting as a medium between
God and the flesh (for it was not possible for the
nature of God to mingle with a body apart from some
medium), there is born, as we said, the God-man, the
medium being that existence to whose nature it was
not contrary to assume a body" (II.6.3).

Origen does not deny the reality of Christ's
body--in contrast to Clement's supposition, it had
genuine need of sustenance (e.g. *In Gal.*, Frag.,
TOLLINTON 1929: 41ff). Yet there remains the sharp
division between divinity and humanity: "God both
like and unlike man" recurs in *Hom. Jer.* xviii.6 for
instance. The thorny problem of the Two Natures is
on view, although not handled with the sophistication
--nor the sophistry--of later generations of theologians (e.g. *In Joh.* xxxii.25, *C. Cels.* I.69, II.9,
etc.). As we saw, Christ's "composite being" allows
some participation in the "ethereal and divine quality"
on the part of his body too. Yet finally the test is
whether *passibility* is a quality of Christ or not.
For body has this quality by definition, since it is
linked with changeability. Later, Gregory of Nyssa
will have to oppose Eunomius strongly on this point,
since the latter claimed that generation involved
passion so that incarnation brought Logos under passibility (e.g. *C. Eun.* IV.1). Origen has posited a

generation of immortal souls or spirits, so that the
focus of the question is shifted to their fall into
bodily existence. As for Logos, he is quite clear
that incarnation means union with a specially prepared
human soul through which even the body is raised to
higher qualities. Yet he can admit a suffering of
Christ's body, and even of his "human soul," insofar
as this does not affect the divine Logos himself.

The transcendent origin of this impassibility
is the eternal generation, according to which the Logos
"was begotten out of the invisible and incorporeal
without any corporeal feeling (*passio*)" (*De Princ.*
IV.4.1). Aristotle's teaching is in mind here, that
the human will involves desire and reason, whereas
the divine will is self-sufficient, without deficiency
and therefore without (the passion of) desire. Yet
when he considers the assumption of soul and body by
the Logos, Origen displays an ambiguity similar to
Clement's. The soul was human and rational, yet
"without feeling or possibility of sin" (*De Princ.*
II.6.5), while the body had been formed without con-
tamination in the Virgin's womb (*In Rom.* 3:8;
QUASTEN: II, 80).

Origen is facing the deep mystery of the
"composite nature" of Christ (*C. Cels.* I.66). He
grants that the Logos intentionally assumed a body
no different from human flesh, "so he assumed with
the body also its pains and griefs" (II.23). Yet he
knows, better than Clement, that his passion and
death are at the heart of divine love and salvation--
he can speak of the "benefit" of Christ's death
(I.54f, 61), and can argue from the reality of his
agonies to the reality of his resurrection (II.16).
His problem is that the divinity of the Logos means
absolute impassibility, so that his entry into
humanity does not allow him genuine participation in
the suffering of the human soul and body he assumed.
Origen agrees with Celsus that we cannot speak of
passion in God, and suggests the method of allegory
to explain contrary scriptures philosophically

(e.g. *C. Cels.* IV.71f). This Alexandrianism is coupled
with the idea of condescension: "the Logos of God
seems to have arranged the scriptures, using the method
of address which fitted the ability and benefit of the
hearers."

Origen is involved in deep contradiction,
which forms the substance of our thesis. He feels
compelled to attribute joy and grief to God, but
"cannot relate this idea to his philosophical-theolo-
gical framework" (R.M. GRANT 1966: 29f; 1967: 15f).
Scholars ever since Charles Bigg have noted in particular such texts as *Hom. Ezek.* vi.6, a remarkable
excursus on the incarnation, as showing the motive
for divine compassion, or *In Matt.* 10:23: "the impassible one suffered by being compassionate." Grant
remarks that in the "very late homily on Ezekiel"
Origen has "finally changed his mind" on the question
of divine passibility. The passage runs: "He descended to earth in pity for the human race. He suffered our sufferings, before he suffered the cross
and condescended to take our flesh upon him. For if
he had not suffered, he would not have come to take
part in human life. First he suffers, then he descends
and is seen. What is that emotion which he suffers
for us? It is the emotion of love. Does not the
Father himself, moreover, the God of the universe,
somehow experience emotion, since he is longsuffering
and of great mercy? Do you not know that when he
distributes human gifts he experiences human emotion?
For 'the Lord your God endured your ways, as when a
man endures his son' (Deut. 1:31). Therefore God
endures our ways, just as the Son of God bears our
emotions. The Father himself is not impassible. If
he is asked, he takes pity and experiences grief,
he suffers something of love and comes to be in a
situation where, because of the greatness of his
nature, he cannot be; and for our sake he experiences
human emotion." This bold attribution breaks with
his usual practice of ascribing emotions to God and
then explaining them away by allegory so that God

remains "completely separate from every affection of passion or change ... unmoved and unshaken forever on that peak of blessedness" (*Hom. Num.* xxiii.2).

Origen's dilemma is that passion or change must involve God in the multiplicity and transitoriness of the created order (OULTON-CHADWICK: 193f on 'Immateriality of God'). Commenting on the phrase of the Lord's Prayer, "Who art in heaven," he stresses the mystical sense as against a "mean conception of God" held by the simple. Ascription of locale to deity leads to "most impious opinions, namely, to suppose that he is divisible, material, corruptible. For every body is divisible, material, corruptible" (*De Orat.* 23). His scriptural material creates not merely a tension with his philosophical theology but indeed an utter contradiction. Perhaps only in such random passages as occur in the later homilies, or in his mystical theology proper, does he allow the divine passion of love to assume a normative role.

Before turning to his comments on the Song of Songs, we may notice one passage notable for its allusion to a difficult saying of Ignatius, and relevant to our present discussion. Origen is discoursing on the meaning of "loving," and the fact that "love" refers to God alone in its strict or proper meaning. "And because God is Charity, and the Son likewise, who is of God, is Charity, He requires in us something like Himself; so that through this charity which is in Christ Jesus, we may be allied to God who is Charity, as it were in a sort of blood relationship through this name of charity ... it makes no difference whether we speak of having a passion for God, or of loving Him; and I do not think one could be blamed if one called God Passionate Love (*Amorem*), just as John calls him Charity (*Caritatem*). Indeed, I remember that one of the saints, by name Ignatius, said of Christ: 'My Love (*Amor*) is crucified,' and I do not consider him worthy of censure on this account" (*In Cant.* Prol., 35). In fact Ignatius was speaking of his carnal passions (*ho emos erôs*, not *agapê*

124

estaurôtai: Rom. 7:2). More important is the question whether Origen's approval at this point has moved beyond the Platonic vision of universal Eros moving all things through desire of The Good. After describing this vision, a team of historical scholars concludes, "It is a tempting picture, and some of the earliest Christian thinkers fell for it. Origen, for instance, seemed so captivated by it that he seems at times quite oblivious to the *agape* which is revealed in Christ" (ARMSTRONG-MARKUS: 89; R.M. GRANT 1966: 31f).

If Origen "seems at times" something different from his appearance at other times, this is probably because he is caught in a historical situation which demands speculative and dialectical thinking, and also because in himself he is creative, imaginative, willing to play his joyful game of interpretation to the limits--and beyond. Thus in this same respect of the historicity of Christ's passion, at times he will extrapolate the passion of Logos into heavenly realms too. He admits that "to seek for this in the heavenly places will seem a bold thing to do," yet in view of heavenly powers of darkness "we should not fear to allow that a similar event also happens there and will happen in the ages to come until the end of the whole world" (*De Princ.* IV.3.13; cf *Hom. Num.* xxiv.1 - SC 460ff). Molland calls this suggestion of *sacrificium duplex* "one of his most audacious ideas," indicating a clear break with Platonic non-historical categories (MOLLAND 1938: 153ff). At the least, it reminds us of the complex and rich texture of Origen's thought, and the risk of reducing it to a system or giving it a label.

(3) MASTER OF THE SPIRITUAL LIFE

The modern revival of interest in "spirituality" has recognized the profound significance of Origen's theology of the spiritual life (QUASTEN: II.94ff; DANIELOU 1955: 293ff; VOLKER 1930; LIESKE; CROUZEL 1961; etc.). Relating the pioneer work of Philo and Clement more explicitly to scripture, he is the real source of Eastern ascetico-mystical theology. The fourth century theorists Gregory of Nyssa and Evagrius Ponticus were disciples, and in the West John Cassian enters the circle through his master Evagrius. Denis the Areopagite was influenced by Gregory although Neo-Platonism is determinative for his work (DODDS 1933: xxvii). Through such followers the Alexandrian spirituality continued its influence, shaping medieval mysticism (Bernard of Clairvaux is Eastern as much as Western) and informing classical theism with its primary idea, the divine anonymity. We shall examine Origen's approach to the spiritual life as well as certain features of his eschatology. Both topics signify the tension in his system between the Platonic dualism of time/eternity and the scriptural motif of present/future.

Stages for Spirit

In his exegetical method Origen had developed what was to be the basis of all future interpretation, the recognition of a manifold sense of the text. Although he claimed to derive this from the LXX of *Prov.* 22:20 ("Have I not written unto you in a triple way?") and from the nature of man as body, soul and spirit (*De Princ.* IV.2.4), he soon proves that he considers the "spiritual" meaning as all important. For the spiritual explanation shows the "heavenly things" of which the scriptural history is "shadow," and the "wisdom" which has been hidden in "mystery" (*Ibid.* 6).

126

As noted, Origen's is not a method of allegory so much as of anagogy, or perhaps mystagogy. Certainly it is the anagogic movement which "leads upwards" from history to spirit that is his concern. Explanation "ascends from the events recorded to have happened to the truths which they signified" (*C. Cels.* II.69).

The spiritual sense of Scripture is the text for the spiritual life of the Christian. The famous example of this is his allegorical interpretation (particularly in the Homilies on Exodus and Numbers) of the Stations of the Wilderness experienced by Israel at the Exodus as the journey of the Christian soul towards perfection. In this he was following Philo and Clement, but in his detailed systematization he shaped the future of mystical theology. He was also giving even greater force to Clement's concept of the image of God, to human perfection as likeness to divinity or "deification" (CROUZEL 1955). The Christian is journeying towards the goal of perfect union with deity, which is not so much a progress into the future as an intensification of his higher nature. The spiritual life begins with the Platonic maxim "Know thyself;" but self-knowledge for Origen means the awareness of being made in the image of God: "The admirable maxim 'Understand thyself' or 'know thyself' ... namely, that thou wast created in God's Image" (*In Cant.* II.5).

The soul struggles to gain *apatheia*, through the practice of detachment. There is already a beginning of mystic vision (*specula*) at this primitive stage of the spiritual life. Then follow trials, accompanied by divine consolation. Even spiritual vision itself may be a temptation; this stage Origen elaborates with keen insight. Indeed, this may be Origen's equivalent to the "dark night of the soul," the lack of which, according to Daniélou, marks a limitation of his theology of the spiritual life: "It is a speculative theory of the way the mind is illumined by the gnosis rather than a

127

description of mystical experience" (DANIELOU 1955: 297). This problem raises the difficult question of the very definition of the mystical, a subject of great moment and controversy today and one to which we will refer in the final chapter. Here we may note that Origen is mapping out man's *way* to God, so that both "ascetic" and "mystical" modalities are involved. He knows the familiar distinction between practical and contemplative, but he knows also their connection: "The way of the Lord is made straight in two ways, according to contemplation (*theôretikon*) ... and to conduct (*praktikon*)" (*In Joh*. VI.11 - SC 157, 103). The good way begins in the doing of justice, and proceeds toward that knowledge of God which in the meantime only the Son enjoys; the end is the apokatastasis (*In Joh*. I.16 - SC 120, 90ff).

When Origen deals with the divine darkness (*In Joh*. II.23), he makes explicit reference to the text which becomes fundamental for mystical theology, *Ps*. 18:11, "He made darkness his secret place, His tent round about him, dark water in clouds of air." He confesses, "if one considers the multitude of speculation and knowledge about God, beyond the power of human nature to take in, beyond the power, perhaps, of all originated beings except Christ and the Holy Spirit, then one may know how God is surrounded with darkness, because the discourse is hid in ignorance which would be required to tell in what darkness he has made his hiding-place when he arranged that the things concerning him should be unknown and beyond the grasp of knowledge." This striking description of the experience of "learned ignorance" in the "cloud of unknowing" is concluded as follows: "I might add a still stranger feature of this darkness which is praised, namely that it hastens to the light and overtakes it, and so at last, after having been unknown as darkness, undergoes for him who does not see its power such a change that he comes to know it and to declare that what was formerly known to him as darkness has now become light."

Origen's conclusion suggests that he is to
be linked rather with Eastern mysticism than with
Western, and that this distinction poses Daniélou's
problem. The Eastern preoccupation with the "uncreated
light" of mystical union, especially as this provides
the key to the Transfiguration story, supports this
thesis. In one passage at least--*De Orat*. 9.2--Origen
speaks of the Christian's eyes gazing aloft in contemplation and even partaking "of a kind of divine
spiritual effluence." Lossky has written, "both the
heroic attitude of the great saints of Western Christendom, a prey to the sorrow of a tragic separation
from God, and the dark night of the soul considered as
a way, as a spiritual necessity, are unknown in the
spirituality of the Eastern Church. The two traditions
have separated on a mysterious doctrinal point, relating to the Holy Spirit, who is the source of holiness
... The one proves its fidelity to Christ in the solitude and abandonment of the night of Gethsemane, the
other gains certainty of union with God in the light
of the Transfiguration" (LOSSKY 1957: 226f).

Origen's O.T. homilies display his exegetical
method and the way it opens the scriptural signs and
types to the hidden truth. Thus Joshua-Jesus reveals
our spiritual combat, the role of anathematized Jericho,
and the nature of the Promised Land. The texts form
a species of runes, as it were, deciphered by the key
of anagogy: *Quae ergo sit ratio sortium*, to adumbrate
the ineffable mysteries (*Hom. Jos.* xxiii.2). Man is
"on the way," his goal is perfection. The way is
mapped out by the Exodus journey--Moses' fourfold en-
campment mirrors four degrees of faith (*Hom. Num.* ii,
iii) but in fact Origen is able to distinguish *forty-
two* stages from the initial travail of the soul and
its flight from bondage, through its temptations and
battles in the desert to the final passage to the
Promised Land (*Hom. Num.* xxvii). This famous Homily
on "The Stations in the Desert" (SC 29, 511ff) shows
Origen's attention to textual detail as well as his
expertise in drawing analogies and allegories. Its
dynamic is the model of the journey, the way of gradual

approach to perfection. The perfect union with God
remains mysterious at the last, for the "river of God"
is approached through the "currents of Wisdom" (SC 29,
555). If at times Origen suggests a union with God
beyond that with Logos or Wisdom, at others he remains
silent before the mystery of spiritual degrees (Mehat
in SC 29: 41ff; VOLKER 1930: 62ff).

The ascetic training, the humbling of the
body, nerves the will to free itself from *pathê*. It
is not unlike the training which Pythagoreans and Platonists enjoin on the immortal soul (*C. Cels*. III.75,
80). The emphasis on bodily askesis is related
negatively to female imagery in scripture, reflecting
a certain misogyny (CROUZEL 1962: 146). Thus the
heroic life of striving after virtue shares in the
traditional one-sidedness of the ideal of "manliness."
Yet Origen's intention is to describe the soul's cultivation of *parrêsia*--liberty to commune with God as
free rather than slave, indeed as son (*In Joh*. I.16).
The difficulty is in large part the result of his in-
dividualism, a problem which the Cappadocians will
have to face seriously (JAEGER 1954: 110f). Origen's
askêsis involves the manifold abstraction we saw in
both Philo and Clement--from bodily passions of course,
but also from those perturbations of mind and soul
which signify insufficient detachment from earthly
ties. The world of appearances, by definition changing
and unstable, continues to exercise power wherever the
athlete has not devoted himself completely to communion
with the unchanging intelligible world. The latter
world is the goal: "A true knowledge of things that
are" (*In Matt*. XII.15; cf *De Princ*. II.11). And it
would seem that the upward path, whether it involves
strict *ekstasis* or not, demands detachment from not
only *things* but also *persons*.

The soul's pilgrimage, according to Origen's
map of the spiritual life, proceeds beyond temptation
to blessedness, leaving the "desires of corrupt nature"
as it approaches "perfect vision." This gnosis
provides a perfect understanding of such divine

mysteries as the incarnation of the Word, and is
characterized by the awesome state that accompanies
such vision: "*Ekstasis*, then, occurs when in knowing
things great and wonderful the mind is suspended in
astonishment" (*Hom. Num.* xxvii.12 - SC 29, 547).
This is one of the two ways in which Philo had used
the term, although it is his other use that became
technical, according to which the human mind is an-
nexed by the divine spirit. For Origen, it is the
contemplative aspect of vision that remains uppermost.
His fullest treatment of the perfect state, in the
Commentary on the Song of Songs, makes this clear.

Origen accepts the Greek-Philonic idea of
three stages in the spiritual journey: purgative,
illuminative and unitive. But whereas Philo had associated these with the Patriarchs, Origen makes a
second and happy association with the three canonical
books of Solomon. He alludes (*Comm., Prol.* 3) to the
three branches of learning, ethics, physics and
"enoptics," which are represented by the books of
Proverbs, Ecclesiastes and the Song of Songs. Origen's
"enoptics" corresponds to Clement's "epoptics;"
Crouzel wonders whether in fact Rufinus' *inspectiva*
is a bad translation so that originally it would have
been the same word. In any case, "L'énoptique (ou
époptique?) origénienne correspond chez Clément à
cette 'époptie des vrais grands mystères' et a comme
elle une signification scripturaire et mystique"
(CROUZEL 1962: 24). The enoptic or "inspective"
science is that which contemplates or beholds
(*theôrein*) "divine and heavenly things." For Origen
this is typified in the figure of Bride and Bridegroom,
teaching us that "communion with God must be attained
by the paths of charity and love." Gnosis is more
than intellectual; it involves an ontological dimension of mystical union (cf VOLKER 1930: 100ff on
Brautmystik).

Origen begins his Commentary: "It seems to
me that this little book is an epithalamium, that is
to say, a marriage-song, which Solomon wrote in the

131

form of a drama and sang under the figure of the
Bride, about to wed and burning with heavenly love
towards her Bridegroom, who is the Word of God. And
deeply indeed did she love Him, whether we take her
as the soul made in His image, or as the Church."
He takes as the theme, therefore, the movement of the
soul in heavenly love as it beholds the beauty of the
Word and receives "a certain dart and wound of love"
(*Prol.* 2). By a strict following of Christ the Way,
there will come a cultivation of the true emotion of
love which he exemplifies (e.g. Second Homily).
Origen is treating of the same "heavenly love" which
qualified his doctrine of divine impassibility. Now
he teaches that to know the Word is to be united with
him in that which is most characteristically divine:
love. He grapples with his old problem, how to distinguish this from "passionate love." He concludes
that only God is Love in the proper sense; love of the
neighbour is a "derived and secondary" meaning, love
of earthly things an "improper" use of the term.

Thus does the soul unite with the Word, in
a "face-to-face apprehension of those things which
formerly we had beheld in the shadow and in a riddle"
(III.5). Here is a final question: how is this perfection related to the consummation? Origen suggests
that in the present life one always needs some shadow,
and that ours is "the shadow of Christ, under which
we now live among the Gentiles, that is to say, the
faith of his Incarnation." But this shadow will be
done away "after the consummation of the age" when we
shall see face to face.

Things Most New

Origen's eschatological teaching is notorious.
It is usually summed up in *apokatastasis* or restorationism (*De Princ.* II.10.8). The question of Origen's
universalism is not our concern here, but rather his
understanding of the consummation of the Christian
life.

As we have suggested, at times Origen seems to teach a consummation through gnosis in the present life. This is evident from his attitude towards liturgy. Liturgy consists of "figurative practices" in which the gnostic, who worships in spirit and truth, participates only "to the end that by such condescension he should bring deliverance to those enslaved by the figure and lead them on to the truth the figure signifies ... The point to note is that not only will true worshippers worship in spirit and in truth in the future but that they are already doing so now" (*In Joh.* xiii.18). In answering Celsus, he makes much of this idea of true worship: "anyone who keeps a feast according to the flesh is not able to keep the feast according to the spirit as well" (VIII.23). It follows that the ecclesiastical hierarchy is not so important for him as the spiritual hierarchy of the Christian gnostic who has advanced beyond the common believer. This is crowned by the ideal gnostic, the *didaskalos*: "The priest who takes away the skin of the victim offered in holocaust ... is the man who removes the veil of the letter from God's word and reveals the members--the spiritual meaning--behind" (*Hom. Lev.* I.4). True worship penetrates through somatic to spiritual Gospel, through the Incarnate to "the Word which, after it was made flesh, rose again to what it was in the beginning, with God" (*In Joh.* I.9). Union with this Word means likeness to God in the divinity which lies behind the accommodative incarnate Word. Here once again we see the tension in Alexandrian thought between the loving God as expressed in the suffering Christ, and the ineffable deity beyond contact with bodily forms and passionate humanity.

Such attainment of deified humanity appears to mean the perfect vision of God in the present life, much as Clement expressed it. It was a conviction of the early Church that the martyr was "made divine by the Word" through union with Christ in his passion (*Exh. Mart.* 25), a union which bestowed impassibility as a foretaste of resurrection. When Origen treats of the consummation of Christian life, however, he is

133

more precise than might have been expected. He takes
quite seriously Paul's analogy of "a seminal word or
reason" (*I. Cor.* 15:35) which, he argues, takes pos-
session of the form of the surrounding substance,
transforming it into its own quality. "Thus is the
ear of corn perfected, excelling beyond comparison
the original grain in size and form and variety"
(*Sel. in Psalm.*, TOLLINTON: 230ff). Therefore the
resurrection body will be "flesh no more," though
the features of the old flesh will remain in the
spiritual body. Elsewhere Origen speaks of a change
in substance after death: the earthly body is patient
of a change in "form and species" so that it will participate in the "unspeakable glory" of the divine
nature (*De Princ.* III.6). This seems as close as he
comes to equating the human eschatological form with
that of the celestial spheres; presumably later
Origenists so interpreted him, leading to Justinian's
charge: "as Origen madly supposes, the body of the
Lord was spherical" (OULTON-CHADWICK: 191, 232, 381f;
cf HTR XLI.2). Origen himself was content to draw on
Platonic teaching (e.g. *Tim.* 33B) and state that "the
bodies of heavenly beings" are spherical (*De Orat.*
XXX.3).

Origen is very careful in his eschatology:
"On this I dare not speak definitely" is almost a
motto. He speculates on the new kind of marriage
which we may expect in the consummation, following his
mystical theology of the Song of Songs (*In Matt.*
xvii.33). He makes a significant application of the
Early Church doctrine of the "eighth day" to the hope
that is in Christ: the new covenant is not "the rest
after the Sabbath" of the old covenant, but a likeness to the crucified and risen Christ (*In Joh.* II.27).

In the light of this teaching, it is not
enough to dismiss Origen as a speculator who demytho-
logized the Biblical eschatology. The burden of his
system seems to do this--the Ascension, for instance,
is a mystical "ascent of the mind" only, since this
alone befits Deity (*De Orat.* 23.2). Yet in general

he is willing to leave his eschatology in suspense.
This is what led Charles Bigg to call him "a true
Ductor Dubitantium, because he knew there was much
that he did not know and yet was not afraid" (BIGG:
130). In his own life Origen was the *didaskalos*,
dedicated wholly to this vocation of teaching the
mysteries of God. As a mystagogue his theology involved "sacred reserve;" this characterizes not only
his eschatology but all his teaching. "I often
think of the maxim: 'It is dangerous to talk about
God, even if what you say about him is true.' The
man who wrote that must, I am sure, have been a shrewd
and dependable character. There is danger, you see,
not only in saying what is untrue about God but even
in telling the truth about him if you do it at the
wrong time" (*Hom. Ezek.* I.11 - cf *Dial. Herac.* 12ff
(149)).

The teacher of doctrine is a reliable guide
only if he is also a master of spirituality. Whatever
Origen's weaknesses, he possessed *style*, the lifestyle
of discipleship, devotion and humility. Even if his
ambiguity left many questions unanswered or badly
situated for future debate, especially the significance
of the incarnate Logos, we can say that his greatness
lies (to apply H.R. Mackintosh' judgment on Schleiermacher) in so discoursing about Christ that the person
of the Redeemer was once again at center stage. For
this reason, perhaps Charles Bigg's words ring true:
"Origen's name has been a kind of touchstone. There
has been no truly great man in the Church who did not
love him a little."

CHAPTER 5

H E R I T A G E   A N D   P R O J E C T

Our thesis claims that Alexandrian philosophical theology exemplified a sort of hybrid, with
Platonic skeleton energized by biblical muscles and
fluids. How far this "Christian Hellenism" was historical necessity is beside the point. The point is
that Christianity--"classical theism" to adopt Charles
Hartshorne's terminology--received a heritage of ambiguity from the Platonism of the Fathers. We have
concentrated on the Alexandrians because they represent
the problem and articulate the heritage in clear and
bold manner. Moreover, they opted for that selective
stream of Greek thought represented by philosophy, an
optimistic rationalism which spurned the "other Greece"
of mysteries and mythopoetic tradition. They set the
stage for theology as abstraction, operating with a
definition of deity which, however noble its moral intention and pure its philosophical credentials, remains
inadequate to carry the weight of the biblical story.
Classical theism proposes an agenda for theology
determined by canons of divine dignity and purity, an
abstract unity and immutable being; in short, the *deus
absolutus* of Olympia, Apollo, Plato and the philosophical *koinê*. The Patristic definition of God is
not wrong because it married biblical tradition to
hellenistic culture: that is not a false move *per se*.
Rather, it has proved unable to break free from
hellenistic presuppositions in order to meet the needs
--a viable theodicy in particular--of both academic
and practical theology today. In this final chapter
we shall illustrate the fate of the Alexandrian heritage, and suggest certain moves which may shift the
balance while honoring the Fathers' intention.

Werner Jaeger has shown that the genius of
the Greek tradition lay in its discovery of the concept of the *appropriate* (JAEGER 1947: 49f). Xenophanes'
critique of anthropomorphic mythology derives from a
religious motivation, a "demand for utter sublimity
in the Godhead." He reduces anthropomorphism to the
absurdity of theriomorphism: "horses would pattern
the form of the Gods after horses, and cows after
cattle, giving them just such a shape as those which
they find in themselves." The concept of "that which
befits the divine nature" (*theoprepês*), coined by
Stoics and taken over by Church Fathers, springs from
the recognition of the unique nature of divinity.
One has to *learn* the divine name just as the Greeks
themselves were said by Herodotus to have received
the names of the gods from the Pelasgians, who had
them in turn from the Egyptians (ROSE).

One discovers what is appropriate to God--
the divine names--by adhering to the canons of transcendent being which were developed by the philosophical schools. One irony of this history is that in
their battle against "anthropomorphism" both philosophers and theologians in fact were guilty of that
very thing, albeit in a sophisticated form. They
imagined divine being as comparable only to intellectual reality, much as Platonism identified *ta asômata*
with *ta noêta*. This philosophy of immaterialism
developed in relation to the moot question whether
the Good, or the ultimate Existent, is beyond being.
Plotinus answered in the affirmative and Neo-Platonism
threw its weight behind the growing emphasis on the
absolute transcendence of God. Whether Clement is to
be called the founder of Neo-Platonism, along with
Numenius, as Bigg does, is highly questionable, as is
any supposition of definite influence on the Areopagite
(BIGG: 253; OSBORN: 187ff). The age of Middle Platonism is not easily distinguishable from that of Neo-
Platonism, historically or theoretically. In the case

of Christian Fathers, both schools are significant, Neo-Platonism more particularly in relation to certain figures such as Origen and Augustine.

The transcendent One of Plato and Aristotle became the absolute God of the Church. Plato had suggested his exaltation even beyond being; Aristotle described the First Mover as indivisible, impassive, unmoved even accidentally. Thus the Christian problem of divine predication became assimilated to the traditional philosophical problem of attribution related to The One, and its answer, the formal classification ascending to negations. Several streams converge. Plato and Aristotle have come together--the dialectic of ascension toward The One has joined with the remotion involved in the science of first principles, which are by definition "immovable" (*Meta.* 1026^a). The *triplex via*, reducible to negations and analogies, places primary weight on negations, for even positive terms are to be interpreted negatively (e.g. "one" means "indivisible"). Philo may have used negations to express divine unlikeness; after Albinus and especially Plotinus they are understood in the Aristotelian sense of negative propositions. It is this development of which Harry Wolfson says, "Plotinus is to be considered the proximate source, though the ultimate source of the entire problem of divine attributes is to be found in Philo" (WOLFSON 1952: 129). Theology itself, once the sense of wonder at the spectacle of divine mystery, *theōria*, is now defined as "first philosophy," the "science of first principles," metaphysics.

The climate of thought was eclectic; "Hellenism" was a way of uniting the chief philosophical traditions, at times substituting theurgy for theory, ritualistic magic for contemplative vision. Of this climate Plotinus is the creative representative and Proclus the systematic. The Neo-Platonic commentators had interpreted Plato's dialectical approach to the One in the *Parmenides* as identical with the theological approach to Deity. This was possible because of their

assumption of the *deus absolutus*, but it also reinforces this concept of the immutable and impassible
God, who is unknown except through highly refined ways
of analogy, negation and mystical union. "Thus, the
sublime masterpiece of Platonic dialectic becomes,
paradoxically, the starting-point of a development
which leads to the medieval and later mystics' conception of God as a 'still desert'" (KLIBANSKY: 25).

Development of Doctrine

          In the stream of orthodox theology the
Alexandrian doctrine of divine impassibility was developed most faithfully: "as against Patripassianism,
Monophysitism and Theopaschitism, the Church as a
whole pursued a course and made distinctions which
were intended to be a safeguard against any ascription
of possibility to the divine nature ..." (MOZLEY: 127).
One must appreciate the positive intention of the
Fathers on this point. The heresies and orthodoxies
of the Patristic era revolve around certain fixed
ideas, notably the one and the many in the doctrine of
the Trinity, and mortality-immortality or possibility-
impassibility in christology. Our thesis concurs with
the judgment of Maurice Wiles that Clement and Origen
had opted for a "mathematical" rather than a "prophetic"
conception of divine unity, thereby directing the doctrine of God into apophatic and even antitrinitarian
philosophical paths: "the mathematical principle of
abstraction carried to the extreme limit" (WILES: 27f).
But we must recognize a parallel problem, expressed
in the christological debates, namely the twofold need
for man to be saved *as* man but *by* God. The Patri-
passian view attempted to guarantee the divine power
in redemption, while following a relentless logic
which involved God in human being. Karl Barth could
say: "there is a *particula veri* in the teaching of the
early Patripassians ... it is God the Father who suffers in the offering and sending of His Son, in His
abasement" (BARTH: IV.2, 357).

This view was complicated by the generally accepted idea of the immortality of souls, which placed man on God's side in ontology; the soteriological thrust was to so unite God with mortal experience as to compromise the essential divine attributes. Thus Gregory of Nyssa quotes Apollinaris as saying, "The death of a man does not destroy death, nor does one who does not rise again. From all of this it is evident that God Himself died, although it was not possible for Christ to be conquered by death." By conflating the two natures in Christ, so Gregory maintained, Apollinaris had "subjected the divinity of Christ to death and was thus propounding the wicked doctrine of the passibility and even the mortality of God" (PELIKAN 1966: 25).

Just as unity and trinity form complementary poles in the doctrine of the Trinity, so the divinity and humanity of Christ suggest a polarity of "natures" that requires a dynamic dialectic to sustain the truth. Whenever it remained static the dialectic suffered the fate of the philosophical logic of abstraction, so that divine impassibility remains isolated from genuine contact with the redeeming work of Passion. And whenever a sense of Christ's oneness as person—the *unio hypostatica*—is developed, as in Athanasius or Gregory of Nyssa for instance, there results a concrete proposal about what must have been his personal experience: "God could not die, but this person who was God did die" (PELIKAN 1966: 27). The ambivalence of the Patristic story provides the horizon for our selection of texts: the depth of the mystery they were contemplating, as well as the several fronts on which they were called to struggle for the truth, made for an inevitable complexity and ambiguity.

Gregory Thaumaturgus, who had honored his teacher Origen by composing the famous panegyric, developed the concept of *theoprepēs* in a treatise on divine passibility and impassibility (QUASTEN: II.127; MOZLEY: 63ff). The treatise begins with the question whether God suffers. A primary difficulty is that if we define God as impassible in nature, we rob him of the freedom to *will* to suffer. Gregory solves this by distinguishing God from man: suffering in God is not the *passio* of human suffering. In divine suffering impassibility is actually revealed, for he wills to immerse himself in sufferings in order to overcome them. Since "in his impassibility he extended his sceptre over the sufferings," God has caused suffering to suffer. Gregory terms him not only "the death of death" but "the suffering of sufferings." Suffering in God "does not occasion any reproach or show any weakness, since the nature of God more excellently displays its changelessness when it is tried by sufferings." Death's failure to hold him shows the divine impassibility, for he destroys the corruptions of suffering in men. The divine immutability, moreover, does not imply inactivity or aloofness, as if he "despised all other things because of the excellence of the rest which he had chosen for himself." Therefore Christ, "remaining what he was, made void sufferings by his impassibility, even as the light drives away darkness."

This treatise indicates the main line of orthodox teaching, which was able to assume divine immutability and impassibility with little apologetic. The sharper problem of Christ's personal suffering was solved by the Two Nature theory. This provided a human mode of passion, while preserving the impassibility of the divinity of Christ. Gregory of Nazianzus could say: "Passible in his flesh, impassible in his Godhead." The communication of the properties was one of name rather than reality (*verbalis communicatio*). The most that could be said of the divine nature of our Lord was that it suffered by compassion with the human nature, or by "sympathy."

Obviously we cannot rehearse the position of many Fathers to illustrate our thesis. There is, of course, the impressive survey of Mozley which leads him to conclude that Fathers, Doctors and Reformers tell the same story: "it is the Arian view of the remote, aloof God, rather than the Athanasian conception of God as truly revealed in Christ, which has prevailed in Christian theology" (MOZLEY: 156). Now Arius built his system "with derelict timber that he borrowed from Origen's woodyard, and twisted in the taking," while Athanasius was "indirectly Origen's disciple" (PRESTIGE: 64). Their dispute concerned what was appropriate to deity. The position of the Tropici whom Athanasius opposed was scriptural to be sure, but their method of choosing analogies was more anthropological than theological. That is, *tropikoi* do not accept the divinity of the Son as *analogans* for the divinity of the Spirit. By arguing from human models or tropes they miss the true proportionality of the biblical imagery. The *homoousios* of the Spirit depends on his essential sharing in what is "proper to the Word" and so "proper to God who is one" (*Ep. ad Serap.* in SHAPLAND: 133). Arius, however, is guilty of reducing language about God to mere homonymity. Athanasius accuses him of faulty presuppositions, allowing him to transpose the divine hypostases "at will, on the analogy of human generation" (SHAPLAND: 187). If the Arian theology, as Mozley insists, carried the day despite history's verdict in favor of Athanasius, it is because the latter cast his orthodoxy in those Platonic categories which were bound to focus attention on abstract attribution rather than the concrete action which he understood so well. Even if it be true that for him the relation between faith and philosophical thinking shows both synthetic and antithetic modes, this champion of the personal activity of God proved capable of interpretation in static terms, and his careful program using Platonic forms was taken to be itself part of traditional Christian Platonism (MEIJERING: 130ff).

Athanasius' *The Life of Saint Antony* suggests the sort of mood which encouraged the ultimate victory of the philosophical tradition over that dynamic trinitarianism for which he had struggled and

suffered. Antony was a "gymnast of God" who took the
apathês Christos as his model (PELIKAN 1962: 99ff).
As Athanasius writes in admiration of the Saint, we
hear the old refrain of the ascetico-mystical path.
After a twenty-year preparation in solitude, Antony
"came forth as out of a shrine, as one initiated into
sacred mysteries ... he had himself completely under
control--a man guided by reason and stable in his
character" (*Vita* 14 - ACW 10, p 32). Antony was
ashamed of eating mere earthly food, and never bathed
(45, 47 - pp 58, 60). His warfare with the Devil is
significant, not least because evil shows an ever-
changing form while the stability of the Christian is
able to appeal to the unchanging victory of the Cross
where "the Saviour stripped them and made an example
of them" (35 - p 49). Athanasius marvels at the number of solitary cells in the hillsides, like a great
choir in unceasing praise, "a multitude of ascetics,
all with one set purpose--virtue" (44 - p 57). Surely
it was this ideal of a spirituality of detachment
which carried the day, despite Athanasius' own valiant
efforts to rescue the Gospel from the Procrustean bed
of the philosophical *koinê*? Relevant to this argument
is the development of catechesis, for example in Cyril
of Jerusalem, until by the fourth century the institu-
tion of Lent had arrived (cf LCC IV, 32). Thus the
festal tradition of the Easter-Pentecost cycle was
displaced by a ritual more attuned to the perennial
philosophy of ascetic negation.

        That this is not the whole story is clear,
not least from the life and times of Athanasius himself and others. Irenaeus, for instance, opposed
the heresies of his time with a bold affirmation of
an authentic incarnation: "neither can it be alleged
that the Son of God became man merely in appearance,
but ... truly and actually" (*C.O.H.* III.18). He
refutes docetic tendencies so explicitly that even
Nygren is led to extol his faithfulness to "the three
fundamental dogmas of the Early Church," creation,
incarnation and resurrection (NYGREN: 121). Nygren
includes Tertullian in his accolade, for he too

insisted that the Word was not merely "transfigured, as it were, in the flesh" but appeared "by a real clothing of himself in flesh" (*Adv. Prax.* 27). Thus orthodoxy for the Fathers meant a non-docetic incarnation of Logos. We do not say that they were self-deceiving, or guilty of bad faith in what we have termed their "ambiguity;" but that their philosophical assumptions jeopardized their "fundamental dogmas." Where the Alexandrian world-view obtained, there the economy of redemption seemed merely an image of the truth.

The Cappadocian Way

The Cappadocians suggest the limiting factor of Platonism, as well as their own struggle to do justice to the dynamic of the Christ-event. Basil and Gregory of Nazianzus prepared the *Philocalia* from Origen's works, and the two *Rules* which were to play a decisive role in the development of Greek monasticism. The impressive career and breadth of interest of Basil reinforce the unity of theory and praxis, and contribute to the general view of classical theism that the best way of knowing and serving God is an ascetico-mystical path. The image of the proper Christian has become, by Basil's time, a solitary soul meditating on divine mystery and committed to severe self-discipline. Of those ascetics whom he met in his youthful journeys after baptism, and who inspired him so much, he writes: "Always, as though living in a flesh that was not theirs, they showed in very deed what it is to sojourn for a while in this life, and what to have one's citizenship and home in heaven" (*Ep.* 223.2 - LNPF VIII, 263).

Gregory of Nazianzus follows suit, but offers along the way a theological methodology, for he is very conscious of "the order of theology" (*Orat.* V.27 - LCC III, 210). Not all men can philosophize about God; only such as are already purified, and "past masters in meditation" (I.3). Converse with God involves

"going up eagerly into the Mount" and entering the
cloud (II.2). A twofold obstacle presents itself,
namely the transcendent nature of God and the obscuring
quality of the material self (II.3). Plato's *Timaeus*
passage is invoked; Gregory comments, "in my opinion
it is impossible to express him, and yet more impossible to conceive" God. Even the "glory" of God, the
Word made flesh and his creative and governing power,
are like the "back parts" which Moses was allowed to
see on the mountain. God is "incomprehensible and il-
limitable," a fact which should not lead to despair
or agnosticism, for "it is one thing to be persuaded
of the existence of a thing, and quite another to know
what it is" (II.5).

Gregory assumes that reason cannot cope with
the unlimited; now God is by definition bodiless. He
is also, therefore, simplex: "every compound is a
starting point of strife, and strife of separation,
and separation of dissolution. But dissolution is
altogether foreign to God and to the first nature"
(II.7). So the familiar cluster of ideas is reaffirmed:
the divine immutability precludes absolute knowledge on
the one hand and absolute involvement on the other.
But the two propositions allow for relative knowledge--
of divine existence but not essence; and relative
involvement--he is "fire and spirit" who purifies the
knower (II.31). In his christology, the image of fire
(and the solar analogy from Plato) recurs, melding
with a host of titles to develop a sort of paradoxology
(III.16ff). The Word could not be generated in any way
involving passion, but undergoes a "lower generation"
as well as the original higher and incomprehensible one
(IV.2). The relation between the two natures remains
paradoxical: "He was tempted as man, but he has conquered as God"; "by the sufferings of Him who could
not suffer, we were taken up and saved" (III.20, IV.5).

Gregory of Nyssa is especially significant
because he brings to fruition the best in Origen (to
give his "Origenism" the benefit of doubt) and because
he articulates the crowning mystical theology in so

146

commanding a fashion. Here again we discern our cluster of concepts—divine name, immutability-impassibility, mystical experience. In combatting the heresy of Eunomius, who reduced the Son to creaturely status, he rehearses the familiar ideas of the unutterable Name of the simplex One, and the titles assumed by the Logos on our behalf (*Adv. Eun.* II.3, III.7, X.1ff and second book, NPNF 290ff). Indeed, like Origen, (*C. Cels.* VI.65) he finds earthly analogies for the divine incomprehensibility--"Let him who boasts that he has grasped the knowledge of real existence disclose to us awhile the nature of the ant" (X.1). The problem of establishing a "passionless generation" for the Son had moved forward to play a crucial role. Eunomius connected generation necessarily with passion; Gregory insists that the incarnation represents "the mystery of the Lord according to the flesh, that he who is immutable came to be in that which is mutable" in order to change it for the better and so abolish the evil with which it was mingled (V.4). Eunomius has rationalized, following Aristotelian categorical logic, the disjunction between attributes of divine and human natures. Christ who suffered must bear a passible nature and therefore could not be eternal deity. This sort of Arian adoptionism is met by Gregory's enunciation of a Two Natures doctrine, so that "the shame of the Passion" is acceptable for orthodoxy through a kenotic christology (V.2f). "What form is it that is buffeted in the Passion, and what form is it that is glorified from everlasting?" (V.5). As God, the Son "is certainly impassible;" it is only "the human element in Christ" which is charged with "the dispensation of the Passion" (VI.1). What will later, in the debates of medieval and Reformation theology, be thrashed out according to concepts of *communicatio idiomatum* and *communicatio verbalis* is here grasped in essence. In his treatise to Ablabius 'That there are not three Gods' Gregory warns against allowing "a customary misuse of language" to govern doctrine and so "to transfer the same error to our teaching about God" (LCC III, 257f).

147

Whatever our judgment about Gregory's contribution to historical theology in these areas of linguistic analysis and trinitarian formulation, there can be no doubt that his primary influence was in the realm of mystical theory. He is the link between the Alexandrians and Denis, Maximus Confessor and Byzantine mysticism (QUASTEN: III.291; DANIELOU 1944; JAEGER 1954: 22ff). "Like is known by like;" as image of God, man can know the Original. But whereas the Alexandrians had tended to emphasize the image of mind, for Gregory the *eikōn* includes *aretē*, indeed makes it decisive. Purity of soul--the symbol is virginity--means a battle against the passions: prelude and path to the vision of God. In this mystic ascent, *apatheia* signifies freedom from slavery to emotion; *gnōsis* involves the night of the senses as the passage from sensible to intelligible worlds is effected; and at last *theōria*, true contemplation is won (C.C. Richardson in LCC III, 239). Thus the classical stages of mysticism are present: purgation, illumination and vision. The initial catharsis of emotions begins a lifelong struggle, the pursuit of manly virtue, issuing in that unitive vision which constitutes authentic *theologia*.

Gregory is Origen's heir, in exploring the three stages of true philosophy, in singling out the Song of Songs as the highest expression of the final stage, and in tracing the "mystical Exodus" through allegorical exegesis of Israel's desert journey. Gregory's *Life of Moses* compares with Origen's *Homilies* on Exodus and Numbers. The *Life* is subtitled "of perfection in terms of virtue" and begins with a simile--like those in Clement and Gregory of Nazianzus--drawn from competitive struggle. The first part of the work is literal exegesis, rightly called *historia;* it soon yields to the long second part entitled *Theōria* (ss 328Aff; SC 1, 106ff). Once again we are invited to contemplate the stations in the desert, manna, the holy mountain, divine darkness, the tabernacle and vestments. A noteworthy section is

that on Moses' vision of God on the mountain (II.219ff-
pp 256ff). The cleft of the rock is a subject for ex-
pansive commentary by Gregory, as he meditates on the
stability which is provided by God alone. Moses plays
the role of seeker with a distinct boldness, the
parrêsia of God's freeman (DANIELOU 1944: 110ff).
Nothing will suffice but the Archetype himself, *to
ontôs on* (231, 235 - pp 264, 268). Playing the role
of president or judge of the Games (*agônothetês*), God
deems him victor and grants the vision. But in fact
Gregory's theme--as he makes explicit in the conclusion
--is that perfection consists in the journey itself.
"The entire life of Moses" is "an example (*hypodeigma*)
of virtue" (305 - p 314). This is so because his is a
continual "spiritual ascension," a constant surpassing
of himself. And at his life's end, Moses has no tomb.
He comes to resemble God in his likeness to incomprehensibility, changelessness and immunity to evil, "a
perfect similitude with his archetype" (318 - p 324).

After the Cappadocians we may note the
homilies of John Chrysostom *On the Incomprehensibility
of God*. Apophatic theology is used here as a weapon
against the Arian revival of Eunomius, "Anomoeism" or
the demotion of Son and Spirit to unlikeness with
Father, *anomoioi*. Theodoret called this "not theology
but technology" because of its technical distinctions
within deity (KELLY: 249). Chrysostom, in his turn,
insisted on the incomprehensibility of the divine
ousia by created spirits, including angelic (*De Incom.*
I.302ff - SC 28, pp 127ff). Not only is God's essence
incomprehensible (*akataleptos*) but also his government,
economy or immanence (I.280f, III.266ff - 124, 208ff).
The essence of the soul is similarly incomprehensible;
indeed, what is happening now is a logical move toward
the idea that the mind cannot comprehend any *ousia* at
all, even what pertains to the creation (II.206ff,
473ff - 161, 180ff). Thus a perennial problem in
epistemology is on view: the nature of the *concept*.

Chrysostom is horrified by the arrogance and
presumption of the Eunomian position, the desire to

meddle and to yield to unbridled curiosity (*perier-gazesthai, polypragmonein*: e.g. I.168ff, 321ff, II.149ff - see SC 28, 129 n5). The Augustinian tradition will term this sort of curiosity a mark of sterile *scientia* as compared with the true (and humble) *sapientia*. Even Greeks were cautious about knowing essential divinity, not daring to rival the folly of the Anomoeist sophisms (V.357ff - p 302). In contrast, John recommends prayer as means toward that true humility which accords with God's ineffable love (V.429ff, 496ff). We are to run to Christ, forgiver of sins and loving judge (V.623ff). So Chrysostom, the preacher's preacher, exhorts those for whom conceptual thinking cannot attain divine truth to turn toward the person of the Redeemer. For him the negations are therapeutic, cleansing us from the pride of intellectualism, in order to reveal the One who waits in love. Such a use of apophatic theology stands in marked contrast to the tradition which would develop through Denis the Areopagite. One might say that there are two sorts of mysticism, one personal and concrete, the other impersonal and abstract. St. John of the Cross distinguished between the "union of love" and the "union of essence," or inclusive and exclusive; the former is Christ-mysticism, the latter the *solus cum solo*. In a theologian such as Meister Eckhart the separation between the two became so radical that the Church was forced to sit in judgment, even if posthumously.

What is decisive is the role assigned to *apophasis*. For Origen there is an apophatic moment in human knowledge of God, but he remains knowable in his essence. The Cappadocians, however, insist that God is essentially unknowable but that through his *energies* we can know him (MEYENDORFF: 70).

The peril attaching to a dialectic of abstraction, for the Church at least, is that of reducing the person and work of the Son so that an absolute unity or *deus nudus* (Luther) is regarded as ultimate. The divine anonymity, accordingly, is no

economic accident but the supreme truth about God.
Thus what is called "the ancient theology" of the
proto-theologians Hermes Trismegistus, Orpheus and
Zoroaster (based on texts dating in fact from the
Patristic period) extolled the anonymity of the abso-
lutely transcendent One (WALKER). It is not so much
Life that is celebrated as the stillness of Death.

The Power of Negative Thinking

The Gnostic doctrine of the Silence which
is next to the Abyss in the Pleroma passed into
Patristic thought as early as Ignatius: "he has.
revealed himself in his Son Jesus Christ, who is his
Word issuing from the silence" (*To The Mag.* 8.2).
The essential character of God was silence, "a
silence broken only at the incarnation, and even then
with reserve and modesty" (C.C. Richardson in LCC I,
80). The quietness of the bishops whom the fiery
Ignatius met at Ephesus and Philadelphia impressed
him as reflecting the divine character of silence
(*To the Eph.*, 6.15).

This concept, however, became more metaphysical and more dangerous as it was caught up in the
general doctrine of the *deus absolutus* indicated above.
For this was agreeable to the age--it was the
Poimandres of the Egyptian esoteric *Corpus Hermetica*
that addressed God as "the Inexpressible, the
Unutterable, whom only silence names." Hermes can
say to Tat, "For in all this nothing exists which
he is not himself. He is both the things that are and
the things that are not ... Such is he who is too
great to be named God ... he has all names because all
things come from this one father, and for this reason
he has no name, since he is father of all." And Mind
addresses Hermes, "If then you do not make yourself
equal to God, you cannot apprehend God; for like is
known by like" (NOCK-FESTUGIERE: I.19, 63f, 155).
The ultimate in this mode was achieved by Gnosticism:

"God is finally separated from his attributes, the Aeons of Reason and Truth, and becomes the Eternal Silence of Valentinus, the Non-Existent God of Basilides" (BIGG: 28; WOLFSON 1956: 522).

Neo-Platonism breathes the same rarefied air of ultimate abstraction, despite Plotinus' own attribution of life to the One. It is his insistence that the One is "beyond being" which provides a final link in the chain of abstraction, as distinct from Middle Platonism. In the *Enneads* we have an authentic intellectualism, making virtue dianoetical, a corollary of *theôria*. The familiar charges of emanationism, even pantheism, at the least indicate the philosophical line Plotinus is attempting to walk. At the end of these meditations appear the famous passages concerning the nameless prodigy, the motionless One. "This is the life of gods and of the godlike and blessed among men, liberation from the alien that besets us here, a life taking no pleasure in the things of earth, the passing of solitary to solitary" (*Enn.* vi.9.11). Such "flight of the alone to the Alone" sums up one way of interpreting the heritage. It reflects itself in Augustine's starting-point: "I desire to know God and the soul. Nothing more? Nothing whatever" (*Sol.* ii.7). For the subtle Augustine that was but one part of the story. He recognized the temptation of the language of negation. Even to say "ineffable" is to say too much: "a thing is not ineffable which can be called ineffable. We should guard against this contradiction in terms by silence, rather than attempt to reconcile them by discussion" (*de doct. Chr.* I.6).

Augustine, of course, knew both sides of the tradition; it is rather in the line from the Neo-Platonist Proclus to the Christian Denis that we see the cold logic of the ascetico-mystical path. Representing the speculative approach of Syrian theology, Denis was to influence medieval thought with ideas of hierarchies celestial and ecclesiastical, and with a theological method which culminates in negation and a crowning mystical union (ROLT: 1ff; DODDS 1933: xxviif;

MEYENDORFF: 68ff). Like Philo, Denis begins with the problem set by scripture, which speaks of God in terms borrowed from creatures that represent him in various ways. To name God from creatures involves theology in a threefold operation. The first moment is affirmative theology, which gives positive (creaturely) names to God, but which cannot give positive content because they apply in a different way to him. Negative theology therefore follows, since "the sacred writers celebrate by every name while yet they call It nameless" (*De div. nom.* I.5). The *Mystical Theology* of Denis thus consists of ascending orders of negatives, concluding with the statement, "It transcends all affirmations by being the perfect and unique cause of all things, and transcends all negation by the pre-eminence of Its simple and absolute nature--free from every limitation and beyond them all" (*De myst. theol.* V). But through his work there emerges a third moment of "superlative" theology which defines God as "super-essential godhead" (*hyperousios thearchia* - e.g. *De Div. nom.* I.5, II.3).

The epistemological formula is simple: human knowledge is limited to the intelligibility of being (a precious tautology); God is hyper-being; therefore he is unknowable. The equation "to be and to be intelligible are one and the same" was stated clearly in Parmenides, and so through Plotinus and Proclus to Denis. It is linked with the idea of exemplarism; of the divine attributes, the differentia are known by *via affirmativa*, the indifferentia by *via negativa* (e.g. *De div. nom.* II.6ff, V.1ff). To pass beyond intelligibility allows the admission of non-existence, in the meontic mode at least, within God (II.7). Denis concludes, according to the dynamic of this remotion, that ignorance is the highest form of knowing God: *Est item divinissimae Dei notitiae, quae per nescientiam accipitur* (VII.3, cf *De Myst. Theol.* 1). Negative theology carries us to the highest reach of thought: what God is not. Beyond that the goal of faith is to continue the ascent to union with That which is revealed in "this Darkness

153

which is beyond Light." Beyond multiplicity, as its source, the One is not so much contemplated as joined: "the Divine Yearning brings ecstasy, not allowing them that are touched thereby to belong unto themselves, but only to the objects of their affections" (IV.13).

The Areopagite touch has shaped the Alexandrian heritage through Neoplatonic categories. Once again we find the divine names reduced to the economy of preparatory steps. This includes Trinity, of course, but even *One* (V, VI, XIII; *De Myst. Theol.* 1). *Thearchia* remains incomprehensible, to be contacted through the threefold ladder of affirmation, negation and ecstasy. Denis may be given benefit of doubt for his obscurity, as Rolt does; or even considered as a spiritual master who deliberately obscures the divine mystery, as Aquinas thinks; or judged one "for whom the impossibility of knowing God was much more attractive and essential than the comprehension of revelation" (KRONER 1959: 132). In any case, through the prestige of Aquinas, whose commentary on *The Divine Names* suggests his estimate, the shaping of classical theism shows the contours of apophatic theology quite clearly.

The last great figure in the procession of Greek Fathers was John of Damascus, who aided the transition to medieval Western Christendom by his handbook on philosophical theology. This would assist the commentators on Lombard's *Sentences,* as well as the Sums of Theology to be written. He includes a eulogy for Denis: *sanctissimus et venerabilis et in theologia praestantissimus vir Dionysius Areopagita* (*De fide orth.* II.3). John begins his statement of orthodoxy with paragraphs on the divine attributes: God is ineffable, incomprehensible, passionless (I.1). Further negations are added: "what he is in his essence and nature is absolutely incomprehensible and unknowable;" God is incorporeal, immaterial, immobile, "moving the universe by immobility" (I.4). He is conscious of the linguistic problem and its doctrinal implications: "alike in the doctrine of Deity and in that of the Incarnation, neither are all things unutterable nor all utterable; neither all unknowable nor all knowable" (I.2). Drawing on Gregory of Nazianzus and Denis, he explains the hard saying of scripture as symbolic, since "it is quite impossible for us men clothed about with this dense covering of flesh to understand or speak of the divine and lofty and immaterial energies of the Godhead, except by the use of images and types and symbols derived from our own life" (I.11). The familiar way of "remotion from all things" (I.4) relates the divine incomprehensibility to the Name of Exodus 3:14. 'He Who Is' signifies that God "possesses and gathers within himself the totality of being, like some infinite and boundless ocean of entity." The figure of *immensum et illimitatum essentiae pelagus*, borrowed from Nazianzus, would become a favorite in the middle ages, not least for Aquinas.

The die was cast: theology was committed to an epistemology in which God is "known" through preparatory discipline of askesis in both thought and life, issuing in mystical union with that Godhead which transcends all. Meister Eckhart could speak of the *negatio negationis*, of a *deitas* beyond the Trinity; and the Church at last decided he was wrong. Theologians had fought shy of saying of the Father that he was more than fountainhead and origin, that he was beyond the persons as an impersonal Ground. But Eckhart does--the Ground is defined as the quiescent "still desert" of *deitas* beyond *deus*. Eckhart follows the logic of the ascetico-mystical path relentlessly, and so is a favorite subject of Rudolph Otto, D.T. Suzuki and others who like to compare oriental and occidental forms of the path. We must transcend time, body and multiplicity to reach God: such detachment or abstraction (*abgeschiedenheit*) approaches "the divine core of pure stillness ... the still desert" of God insofar as it approximates that nothingness "before God produced creatures" (*Von. Abg.*; Sermons 2, 4, 15 etc - BLAKNEY: 82ff, 107ff). Thus he speaks often of the "silence" or "dark" or "unconscious"

which characterizes the soul's approach to God
(e.g. LCC XIII, 180ff). Rather than remaining with
a relative concept of ineffability--so runs Lossky's
judgment, comparing him with Augustine--Eckhart
pushes it to the absolute limit. Thus his apophatic
method, like that of Denis, is not content with a
dialectic of polyonymy and anonymy but ranges the
two in a process in which the anonymity of deity is
ultimate (LOSSKY 1960: 15ff, 60ff).

The heritage of ambiguity of which the
Alexandrians are typical if not causal comes at last
to the *via negativa*: a learned ignorance launched
into the cloud of unknowing. Its intention was excellent, for Fathers and Doctors sought to honor what
is appropriate to God by setting every positive statement about him in parentheses. Every analogy by definition means "likeness" and *therefore* "unlikeness."
When Aquinas developed the Aristotelian concept of
analogy in its "theo-logic" he settled on the analogy
of "proper proportionality" to carry the burden because of its safeguards, its qualifiers (*S.T.* I^a,
13.4ff; *S.C.G.* I, 13-34; Cajetan, *De Nom. Anal.* 3.24).
Only when the mistaken analogy of "proportion" rather
than "proportionality" is on view--as in Eckhart--can
theological symbolism forget its limits on *both* sides
of the equation. Then, against the lure of anthropomorphism, one presses the negation so far that the
positive lapses and the temptation to agnosticism is
on view.

Clement of Alexandria was well aware of
symbolism in non-Christian as well as Christian litera-
ture (e.g. *Str.* v.IVff) while Origen developed the
idea of accommodation to handle the problem. Bigg
thought that by the latter, "the key was in the lock"
for solving scriptural anthropomorphism, although it
was reserved for later ages to turn it (BIGG: 147).
What they intended to make clear was that both anthropomorphism and anthropopathism are verbal symbols,
improprieties of language, related to the divine
paideia. As apostles of the divine blessedness and

perfection, they chose weapons of immutability and impassibility. But their defence created its own mythology, of divine ineffability and human *theôsis* which slanted the Gospel toward that perennial philosophy which could but demythologize its historicity. In their zeal for the divinity of God they could not find proper place for the humanity of his Word, and for the test case of Christ's suffering. For them, "passion" is so fixed in relation to that which is mutable that they could not entertain a concept by which the immutable might engage in a Passion not only of his own choosing but consonant with his aseity. That would have spelled the end of their philosophical world-view. That they could not make such an end is no great wonder; rather are we to blame if we prove unable to follow the leading of alternative models of the divine.

Classical Theism and the Crucified God

The debates of the Fathers are not so easily reduced to definitions and party-lines as polemical theology used to imagine. There is, as J. Pelikan so well reminds us, the question whether the conceptual history beloved of scholars is as reliable a guide to the past as the history of those "beliefs and practices" which form the perennial substance of faith (PELIKAN 1969: 32). The Chalcedonian formula may seem exemplary, for its sacred reserve made do with a careful series of negations in regard to what Bonhoeffer termed the *Wie-frage* of christology. Yet it seems clear that the Platonic *apatheia* "constitutes the a priori presupposition" of patristic ideas of God on *both* sides of the Monophysite controversies (ELERT: 71ff).

By the fifth century the crucial problem for Christian theology was *theopaschism*. The terms of the debate were consequent upon the Chalcedonian struggle between Nestorian and Eutychean christologies; but meanwhile the Chalcedonian statement had provoked a Monophysite reaction. The question was, who is the subject of the Passion? Monophysite objectors to the Creed--they found a home in 6th C. Alexandria--argued for a body of single nature, hence incorruptible. They could appeal to an apparent ambiguity in Athanasius as to whether resurrection preserved the body from corruption or simply signified its essential incorruption (*De Inc. Verbi* 21ff). So there developed a party-strife between Phthartolatrae and Aphthartodocetae. E.R. Hardy comments: "Under these strange terms there lies the crucial question, Was Christ a real man?" (LCC III, 34). The problem was that the distinction of natures (as expressed in Leo's Tome) required qualification to save it from a Nestorian interpretation: the unity of Christ's person seemed in doubt. Leontius of Byzantium had suggested the formula "one of the Trinity suffered in the flesh," at first rejected but later accepted by the Fifth Ecumenical Council (II Constantinople, 553 - LCC: III, 375; cf MANSI: IX.383). Thus did the Monophysite position appear less extreme, more like a demand for working out the logic of *unio hypostatica*. "So out of the tradition of Greek philosophical theology itself comes a repudiation of the philosophical assumption of the utterly impassible deity" (Hardy in LCC: III, 35).

John Meyendorff's fine analysis of Eastern christology shows the crucial role of Cyril of Alexandria's theopaschite formulae in the debate between Chalcedonian and Monophysite; "only *someone* can die, not something, or a nature, or the flesh" (MEYENDORFF: 52). This more appropriate lead struggled against the axioms of immutability and impassibility, as various christologies searched for less improper ways to express Gospel (PELIKAN 1971: 247ff). Beyond Chalcedon, for instance, was the subtle reasoning of II Constantinople on the twin concepts of *anhypostasia* and *enhypostasia*: Christ's humanity has no existence on its own, anhypostatic, but is enhypostatic within the incarnation (BARTH: I.2, 163ff).

The significance of such christology is that it assumes an ontology in which there can be genuine commerce between divine and human, without either confusion or absorption. Rather than a simple fusion of "two natures" we see a hypostatic union which involves a "representative" or model humanity, both example of authentic human being and power to heal and enable our participation in that being. This "dissymetric Christology" reflects a step beyond Chalcedonian apophatism, in the East at least, where ideas of participation and theosis prevailed (MEYENDORFF-McLELLAND: 19ff, 149ff). The conclusion can be made "that God is not only an immutable and imparticipable essence but also a living and acting Person. By assuming humanity hypostatically, the Logos 'becomes' what he was not before and even 'suffers in the flesh'" (MEYENDORFF: 120, 164). Herbert Richardson sums up the development of dogma: "To conceive God to be such that He cannot be present *in* Jesus of Nazareth, but only through Him, is the characteristic of 'Hellenism.' This Greek attitude assumes that God's divinity is a nature (or essence) which is, in principle, incapable of being in the world ... At II Constantinople Hellenism was overthrown and the question left unanswered by Chalcedon was settled: Jesus Christ, the subject of the two natures, is Himself God in person" (RICHARDSON: 135f).

Despite the theoretical advance, one wonders whether christology was indeed freed from the essentialism of the Greek tradition. For instance, an unhappy anthropological corollary seems clear: the "masculinization" of the ascetico-mystical theology. Thus a discussion of Evagrius provokes the comment, "The ascetic movement as a whole suffered from an extravagant horror of feminine society" (O. CHADWICK: 54). Evagrius had stressed the negative mood of apathy and *ataraxia*, although Cassian's translation gave the West a somewhat more positive vocabulary. Yet even this theoretical advance, Chadwick concludes, sanctions "as thoroughgoing a practical dualism as it is possible to conceive within the limits of a still Christian thought" (O. CHADWICK: 90).

Here is a "project" indeed for modern scholarship, to trace the tragic story of that misogyny which haunts classical thought. Involved are elements deriving from the primitive struggle between earth-mother and sky-god, the "dyadic" contest enlightened by the researches of Mircea Eliade and Joseph Campbell, for instance; other elements carry over from that "optimistic rationalism" suggested as the philosophical heritage, which interpreted the virtues in masculine terms and insisted on a sharp dichotomy between reason and passion in the very definition of virtue (*vir*, *virtus*). The contemporary problem of "gender identity" has a long history, one with considerable significance for the fate of classical theism. It would be of interest to attack the problem through comparison of alternative creation myths, e.g. those of Genesis and of the Greek tradition. Charles Williams, for instance, was well aware of the threat to the popular androgynous myth posed by the biblical category of the created couple, "the Adam" (SHIDELER: 45ff).

Thus the development of dogma--whatever one's estimate of Harnack's thesis on hellenization-- involved a distinct degree of "de-judaization." For the O.T., the changelessness of God had been a theological-moral confession rather than an ontological statement: God is trustworthy in his covenantal relationships. But through subsequent speculation immutability "assumed the status of an axiomatic presupposition for the discussion of other doctrines," resulting in "a Pyrrhic victory" over Greek philosophy inasmuch as the latter's ontological axioms continued to shape orthodoxy (PELIKAN 1971: 21ff). We need to recover the intentionality of the Patristic doctrine: the negative prefixes "really testify to divine freedom and independence" (PRESTIGE: 4). Immutability asserts God's trustworthiness, impassibility his moral transcendence, anonymity his eminence beyond our linguistic and conceptual categories.

The problem is clearest when we consider the doctrine of "the crucified God." Classical theism was able to solve the apparent paradox by appeal to its Platonic ontology: the separation of spiritual and material. This meant that salvation consists in an escape from the pull of matter, through the instrumentality of Christ's soteriological office and work. But the latter could not be more than instrumental, since flesh participated in the meontic pull downward. "Genesis is the beginning of corruption" said Philo; "Passion is the fountain of sins" (*Doc. Orac.* 12; *Quod Deus* 72). For the Alexandrians in particular the divine "will" consisted in the recovery of man's theosis through victory over the negative power of evil. This form of what Aulén has called the "classic" theory of atonement provides a place for the Passion, but in terms of an economy of gnosis which transcends it (FLOYD: 21ff; DANIELOU 1955: 40ff; KOCH: 99ff). Since revelation means gnosis, salvation is rather noetic than soteriological; the stress on freedom of the will suggests the moral vision which allows the soul to make its ascension. Providence is more significant than salvation, for the divine paideia guides the soul to that *theologia* which means esoteric knowledge and ontic unity (*henôsis, theôsis*).

Such gnosticism may take subtle forms, expressed in the profound language of devotional paradoxology: "How, then, art thou compassionate and not compassionate, O Lord, unless because thou art compassionate in terms of our experience, and not compassionate in terms of thy being" (Anselm, *Prosl.* 8). The world-view informing this prayer is based not only on the classical dichotomy of matter and spirit but also on the assumption that the reasoning of faith or *fides quaerens intellectum* is able to begin from above, from the divine *quoad se* and move analogically downwards. Today's post-critical philosophy would insist on reversing this direction on behalf of theological anthropology, "from below."

The thrust--if not caricature--of "classical theism" has provoked a stimulating response during the past century and more. It may be that history had to await the demise of classical theism through its own inner development as Deism. The rival philosophies of modern Europe, rationalism and empiricism, are described by Walter Kaufmann as "philosophies of revolt" against theism (KAUFMANN: 20ff). They reflect the logical extension of the *deus absolutus* and his remoteness from the created order--from "reality!" Remotion posed increasingly the problem of theodicy--on display in the wrestlings of Hume, Leibniz and Kant: if God is both all-powerful and all-loving, then why evil? As Kant saw, thus formulated the "problem of evil" is insoluble and theism falls. Like Pascal before him, he recognized the necessity of escaping the logical impasse of theism, of developing a dialectical method appropriate to a knowledge of God both risky (lacking certainty) and objectively grounded (possessing certitude)(cf GOLDMANN: 235ff). Such an epistemology, traceable from Clement of Alexandria to J.H. Newman, offers a grammar of assent that honors the humanity of both knower and known in the relationship of faith. Yet it seems only recently that theologians have recognized that Christian Hellenism is helpless to provide appropriate concepts for the phenomenon of the crucified God and of the human faith responsive to it. We cannot but note some of the witnesses, who offer not merely a radical challenge to classical theism but also the *project* for theology today. This programmatic conclusion involves two main criticisms, concerning the divine Passion and the divine Name.

The first criticism, on behalf of the crucified God, has teased the theological imagination of the twentieth century. In the early decades a debate was sparked, symbolized by the famous essay of Baron von Hügel and the historical survey of J.K. Mozley (VON HUGEL, MOZLEY). B.R. Brasnett's synthesis of 1928 sums it up: *The Suffering of the Impassible God*. Data on the divine passion were assembled from scripture (e.g. ROBINSON) and historical theology (e.g.

FAIRBAIRN), while on the philosophical side William James and Edgar Brightman argued for a limitation in deity to account for the fact of evil and the need for divine suffering. The classical emphasis on abstraction and the consequent distinction among divine attributes was countered by a concern for the covenantal and manward attributes so prominent in scripture (MOZLEY: 127ff; MEIJERING: 148ff). A recent study has illustrated the shift in reference to recent theologies, especially that of Karl Barth and his analogy of faith, so consonant with the biblical centrality of *Agape* (LEE: 6ff, 91ff).

Karl Barth exemplifies the new mood--doubtless linked to what Franz Rosenzweig termed "the new philosophy" of personal encounter--by stressing the *Mitmenschliche* nature of being, divine as well as human, and the impossibility and scandal of attempting to describe God in isolation from his relationship with man (e.g. BARTH: IV.1, 157ff, 'The Way of the Son of God into the Far Country'). Despite the problems raised by such *Offenbarungspositivismus* it secures the person of Jesus Christ and the consequent necessity to do theology according to the christological paradigm (McLELLAND 1974: 42ff). Thus what Barth calls "the very special dialectic of the revelation and being of God" means a commitment to "the order intrinsic to the theme," an objectivity following the signs of that divine being which is to be interpreted from the divine acts (BARTH: II.1, 348ff). Whatever one's estimate of Karl Barth, it seems clear that a crucial element in modern theology shares this insight into the failure of classical theism--that is, of Hellenistic ontologism --to provide categories adequate to biblical realism. This had been Philo's problem too: his final word is negative, the bare positing of The One; but in order to take his Bible seriously he "is therefore bound to conclude that the positive content of the doctrine of God is derived from revelation" (CHADWICK 1967: 149).

It is Charles Hartshorne who has waged an explicit and concentrated attack on what he calls

"classical theism"--giving pride of place in the
latter's development, we should note, to "Philo the
Founder" (HARTSHORNE-REESE: vii, 2ff, 76ff).
Hartshorne's is a religious philosophy which develops
the metaphysics of Whitehead, especially the critique
of traditional transcendence/immanence (WHITEHEAD
1933: 169ff) and the concept of "dipolar" deity involving both primordial and consequent poles within
the godhead (WHITEHEAD 1929: 403ff). Hartshorne's
own developed "panentheism" claims to be an exposition of the text "God is love" and his analysis of the
divine attributes substantiates his claim that classical theism failed to recognize their *social* nature
(HARTSHORNE 1948: 116ff). His dipolar theism appeals
to the law of polarity over a theology of *actus purus*
or "monopolarity" and notes the logical entailment
of relativity: "To be independent, absolute, is to
be meager in logical content; the maximum of relativity is the maximum of logical content" (HARTSHORNE
1948: 95). So "process thinking" is able to relate
the eternal with the temporal in a way free from the
embarrassment of classical thought, and even to establish the appropriately divine in just such relatedness. Its dialectic of being and becoming, to be sure,
is open to the accusation of immanentism and even
determinism. In this regard it requires qualification
--for example: "Being is not in balance with becoming.
Being comprises becoming and rest, becoming as an implication of dynamics and rest as an implication of
form" (TILLICH: I.247). Such a brief sketch cannot do
justice to process thought or to Tillich's rather different theology; yet it points to contemporary onto-
logists who criticize the classical tradition along
the very lines this book has followed. Of other
voices on this point of divine attribution we will
mention two: Kitamori and Moltmann.

Kazo Kitamori brings a worthy passion to his
theme, appropriately entitled "the pain of God."
Drawing on biblical texts such as Jeremiah 31:20 and
Isaiah 63:15, he develops a theology in which "The
fact of the cross is the axiom of theological thought,"

providing an *analogia doloris* (KITAMORI: 47, 56,
151ff). It is significant that he consciously opposes
his "mysticism of pain" to the "mysticism of suffering"
associated with classical theism. He considers the
latter to be a form of self-hatred which strives after
a higher pleasure through "inner will power." This
form of hedonism, he maintains, lacks the power of
Deus crucifixus, just as the traditional concepts of
ousia and *substantia* produced "an essence without
essence" because God lacked the divine pain which con-
stituted his reality in the biblical covenants
(KITAMORI: 46, 77ff). Such a theology of the pain of
God reminds us that theology and anthropology are correlative. A world-view in which "the emotions are regarded as essentially hostile to the soul's apprehension of the good" (MOZLEY: 59) will necessarily see
God as the good beyond passion. This is so because
its formal logic defines passion as the capacity to
be acted on by another, and therefore the capacity for
pain. Hence a divine "passion" or "suffering" is un-
thinkable since God is separated by an infinite gulf
from such capacities. So long as essential being
denotes that which transcends created body it will
prove impossible to grant genuine suffering to God.
And so long as God is defined in terms of being it
will prove necessary to develop a supranaturalism to
describe his eminence. The world-view of classical
theism cannot reflect that of biblical faith without
distortion on this decisive issue, the pain of God.

Jürgen Moltmann, noted for his theology of
hope, recently articulated "a trinitarian theology of
the cross" or *der Gekreuzigte Gott*. Moltmann's
starting-point suggests the new context for doing
theology today: "suffering precedes thinking." In
one sense it is the perennial question, concerning
innocent suffering, which the classical world took
seriously too. But whereas that world began from a
general sense of a transcendental answer, an idealist
reconciliation, today's theologian is committed to
history. For him, theodicy faces not the puzzle of
"privative" evil but the harsh reality of the Holocaust

--not merely suffering to a higher degree but such a monstrous evil that our classical theology is shaken. Moltmann recommends as "answer" a prior reflection on Christ's suffering, not least his forsakenness. This phenomenon, his analysis suggests, could not be explained in traditional terms, because of "the inadequacy of the doctrine of the Two Natures" (MOLTMANN: 200ff). The influence of Ernst Bloch's critique of Christianity is apparent, for the Marxist charge of theological opiate describes too much of classical theism to be dismissed lightly. Moltmann recognizes in Bloch's "atheism for the sake of God" a legitimate demand for a theodicy which will not abandon the good creation through an other-worldly eschatology. Therefore he moves into a close analysis of the concept of *apatheia* in order to develop a theology of hope which will be an authentic extension to a theology of the Cross (MOLTMANN: 267ff). Thus Luther's demand for *theologia crucis* proves a valid insight into the decisive axiom of Christian faith, and the radical departure from classical theism it implies for the doctrine of God, the *theo-logia*.

A Name for God

The idea of "God the anonymous" represents the convergence of several streams of historical thought. Our conclusion wishes to point up the ambiguity of this heritage, and the correlative complexity of our modern project. Ambiguous heritage and complex project: are things quite that bad? Yes, if we are to judge by the innumerable analyses of contemporary "crises"--of faith, of authority, of confidence, etc. With Christians self-consciously in the minority and theology on the defensive, what are the options? One is to make faith adjectival rather than nominal: Christian humanism or secularism or marxism. Another is to relativize faiths in a radical comparativism: different paths ascend the same mountain; all divine names are valid. Max Müller held that the names of divinities in world religions resulted from a "disease of language" which substitutes *numina* for *nomina*--inflating ordinary names to religious powers, or poetic to theological speech. The question of why divine names are holy and unspeakable (cases of reserved words, such as the vocative of *anax*, and royal tongues applied to gods alone) presents a perennial puzzle to students of religion--Müller, James Frazer, Robert Graves for instance. We have seen that the Alexandrians were far from naive about the logical status of religious language, anticipating much of the vaunted breakthrough of modern philosophy into "linguistic analysis." They also display an exemplary openness to discuss Christian theology in the context of "religion" as well as in relation to the mysterious role of the imagination, root of the icons of our thought and language.

On the Day of Atonement the Jewish high priest pronounced--this single time in the entire year --the ineffable name of God. In biblical studies today the Tetragrammaton may provide a focus for linguistic analysis. The Uppsala school as well as E.O. James have drawn on Andrew Lang's High God theory or *deus otiosus*: Moses revived El's otiose name Yahweh to denote the covenant-God of his people (JAMES 1935: 83ff). Albright's study of YHVH, in its grammatical form as causative verb, cites Egyptian and Accadian analogues for the hiph'il construction "He causes to be what comes into existence" (ALBRIGHT: 197ff). Jewish scholars, notably those associated with the Patmos circle which stressed the Johannine logos as interpersonal dialogue, attended to the peculiar significance of assigning a personal name to deity. Franz Rosenzweig contrasted the timeless "thinking" of classical tradition with the "speech-event" of the new philosophy: "Speech is bound to time and nourished by time, and it neither can nor wants to abandon this element" (STAHMER: 148). His interest in the medieval poet Juda-ha-Levi illustrates further Rosenzweig's insight into the doxological nature of biblical theology. One of the poems he translated was *Yah Shimka:*

"O God, Thy Name!" Another much influenced by the
O.T. was J.G. Hamann, who spoke of gnawing on the
word, the "bone of language." Martin Buber stressed
the exclamatory nature of the Name; perhaps the simple
ya ("Oh!") evoked by numinous encounter developed into
Ya-huva, "O-He!" (BUBER: 48ff). Such concerned speculation would strike Daniélou as sound, for there was
probably "another line of theological thought, parallel to that of Philo, but with the Name not the Logos,
as its focal concept" (DANIELOU 1964: 147ff).

Obviously the divine name is a topic opening
on the whole of theology, and patient of all the
variety possible in handling such a subject. The classical view of proper names, for instance, derived from
Plato a "no-sense" theory as it is called, still present in Wittgenstein's writings, and opposed by a
rival theory, of Frege and others, which proposes that
proper names possess a certain sense (*Sinn*) (EP:
VI.487ff). The activity of naming thus introduces
the thorny problem of predication or attribution,
traditionally approached through the hellenized "metaphysics of Exodus" as Gilson terms the classic interpretation of Exodus 3:14. When Thomas Aquinas dis-
cusses the question *Utrum hoc nomen Qui est sit maxime*
nomen Dei proprium he assumes the tradition we have
been examining, that the problem *de nominibus Dei* can
be solved by denoting God as 'He Who Is'--along with
the corollary that the divine essence remains unknowable (*S.T.* I, q. 13, a. 11; cf q. 3, prol.).
Meanwhile, in Jewish theology, the Kabbalists made
much of the distinction *deus absconditus, deus revela-*
tus: God in himself remains *'En Soph*, "That which is
without limit" (not even negations are allowed), while
through the powers which emanate from That (the ten
Sephiroth), both acts and even emotions have place
(cf GUTTMANN: 224f).

The history of the concept of *analogy* illustrates the struggle of Latin theology to handle divine
predication. That history represents no mere capitu-
lation to Aristotle's formal "ana-logic" so to speak,

but rather an attempt to honor the dynamic content of Gospel in light of the Philosopher's categories. The resulting "theo-logic" steers Aquinas to opt for the analogy of "proper proportionality," substantiating what Barth will later term the "exegetical decision" for the *analogia fidei*, taken "under the compulsion of the object" of faith (BARTH: II.1, 227). The Occamist line proposed a refinement and tension, holding that human statements are only about *concepts* during the present life.

The Reformation was part of the history of the doctrine of analogy, in the sense that it shared in the nominalist-realist debate, while pressing the issue of biblical analogies to the limit. Luther's stress on the hiddenness of God, for example, is far from the classical remotion associated with that *deus nudus* which he rejected so harshly; instead he draws on the Occamist theory of linguistic impropriety to show that in revealing himself, God conceals himself. So also in Calvinism: Calvin has constant reference to the *improprietas* of theological speech, developed by such a colleague as Peter Martyr, even though the latter looked more to Aristotle than Plato in working out his concept of analogy (McLELLAND 1957: 74ff; cf BARTH: II.1, 225ff). That is, the Reformed way of interpreting the classical tradition was to accept the formal logicality of the doctrine of God (conceived in the static terms of Christian Hellenism's ontology) while qualifying the substantive categories with more dynamic or active analogies from scripture. The primary example is christological, where the two natures theory of the *person* is presupposed, but qualified by the stress on the active *work* in death and resurrection. This seems evident from that controversy which in fact dominated the sixteenth century scene on all fronts: Christ's presence in the eucharist. Here indeed the true issue was joined: is there a divine Agent in *active relation* to human acts and relationships?

The debates within Neo-Thomism used to argue about the significance of St. Thomas' "silence" (Josef Pieper) and of his "existentialism" (Maritain). Now that transcendental Thomism has taken account of Kant's "critical shift" there is a more radical debate, associated with Karl Rahner's investigations and Leslie Dewart's programmatic books. The "future of belief debate" revolves about a similar thesis to ours: "the integration of theism with today's everyday experience requires not merely the *demythologization of Scripture* but the more comprehensive *dehellenization of dogma*, and specifically that of the Christian doctrine of God ... hellenization introduced into Christianity the ideals of immutability, stability and impassibility as perfections that all Christians and Christianity as a whole should strive for, since these were the typical and central perfections of God himself" (DEWART 1966: 49, 134). Dewart's project is not the negative one involved in "development of dogma" but the positive resulting from the "underdevelopment of theism." By the latter he means that the adoption of hellenistic categories, including the Parmenidean identification of being with intelligibility (recalling Heidegger's charge which we noted in beginning the present work), fated Christian theism to the problematics of essence/existence and the consequent definition of God as supernatural being (e.g. DEWART 1969: 139ff; cf DUMERY 17ff, 78ff). Much in Dewart's work has aroused indignation and rebuttal. Pelikan, for instance, claims that "the trinitarian and christological dogmas were as much a fundamental refutation of hellenism as they were some sort of 'adaptation of hellenic concepts'." Despite his criticism, however, Pelikan acknowledges "the unavoidable conclusion that the orthodox christology of two natures in one person is an underdeveloped doctrine" (PELIKAN 1969: 28, 68; cf LONERGAN).

What is at issue in the debate is the Christian view of *history*. The hellenistic approach tends to cast a certain ambiguity about the reality of historical existence, being-in-the-world --the logic of assigning authentic existence to a historical being. Thus the attributes of historical existence include mutability, the characteristic of that which is derivative: only the created is subject to change (NORRIS: 145ff). The phenomenon *naming* is linked to this idea that the begotten is dependent and therefore mutable, as the act of receiving a name from another signifies (PANNENBERG: 150f). This cluster of ideas has played a major part in historical theology, especially in working out doctrines of the Fall and Original Sin.

The "project" we are submitting has been further promoted by the short-lived but nonetheless significant "God is Dead" movement in recent American theology. Here the question seemed to be whether some actual Being has suffered ontological change (Altizer) or whether it is the religious and cultural Name that has proved problematic for a new generation (William Hamilton). Two influential books, Harvey Cox' *The Secular City* and Leslie Dewart's *The Future of Belief*, close with a call for "a moratorium on speech until the new name emerges," "to reserve a special place for *silence* in *discourse* about God" (COX: 265ff; DEWART 1966: 212ff). Both seem to be making the same point, that since "God" has become a proper name and since God-talk has now so little value for so many, apologetic theology should attempt the task of connoting rather than denoting, rather like Kierkegaard's project of "indirect discourse."

Such guidelines for doing theology today reflect not only a reaction to classical theism but in fact a positive response to the Patristic appreciation of apophasis. Jacques Maritain's analysis of the "degrees" of human knowledge relates negative theology to mystical. He takes St. John of the Cross as typical of the latter; his formula *todo y nada* (All and Nothing) stands in contrast to the Alexandrian insistence on an intellectual knowledge of God, in which even apophatic knowledge must "remain intellectual in mode" (MARITAIN: 236ff). Similarly, Karl

171

Barth has commented on the Fathers' statements about the divine ineffability: they "knew almost too well and said almost too eagerly that we speak of God humanly and therefore inadequately when we do so in sensible expressions" (BARTH: II.1, 227ff). He notes that "anthropomorphism" applies as much to "spiritual" conceptions of the divine as to bodily ones. He warns against mistaking the *ineffabile* of human spirituality for the genuine ineffability revealed in the divine condescension. For Barth the anthropomorphic language of scripture describing God's gracious *approach* to man expresses the divine *distance* more forcibly than abstract concepts of transcendence. He is seconded by Bonhoeffer: "The abstract concept of God is fundamentally much more anthropomorphic just because it is not intended to be anthropomorphic, than childlike anthropomorphism" (BONHOEFFER: 43).

Karl Barth was arguing for the reversal of the classical order of trinitarian speculation, which began with divine being in general and proceeded to the triune nature. He considered this a species of nominalism, "for the order undoubtedly implies that it is a question first of what the being of God is properly in itself, and only then of what it is improperly in its relationship *ad extra*" (BARTH: II.1, 349). This shift is supported by the contemporary Roman Catholic theological renewal, which may be described as a displacement of the substantive categories of "classical man" by *relational* categories. Karl Rahner, as an outstanding example, scores traditional "anti-Trinitarian timidity," for "if one starts from the basic Augustinian-Western conception, an a-trinitarian treatise 'on the one God' comes as a matter of course before the treatise on the Trinity" (RAHNER: 13, 18). He insists on the identity of "immanent" and "economic" Trinity, charging that the classical dichotomy is a virtual "monotheism." The contemporary debate--one should mention Schoonenberg as well--has been described as "christology from below", approaching its subject through anthropology, or better through the humanity of Christ and so through

his identification with us. Classical thought began
with deity: its problem was to achieve a concept of
incarnation against the lure of docetism; ours today
begins with humanity, and our temptation is adoptionism. Yet our game of "naming the whirlwind" under-
stands well that apophatism has burdened classical
theism with its risk of agnosticism (GILKEY; BRUNNER
1949: 128ff).

Transcendence is a concept that has suffered
much from its friends, who thought to safeguard the
religious intentionality by exalting the divine by
means of privations, negations and contrasts. The
ordo cognoscendi was to be surpassed in an *ordo essendi*
conceived as utter abstraction, extending divine essence beyond thinking and even being. So there followed the unhappy history of succeeding attempts to
find appropriate language for the biblical claim that
something happened along Israel's way. Now if analogy
is, as Barth puts it, "the correspondence of the unlike,"
then the divine accommodation must not be itself "transcended," else the analogical relationship is declared
merely a pedagogical device. We saw how this operated
in the Alexandrian world-view, and how that sort of
transcendentalism denied proper being to the human
emotions, indeed to man-in-history.

Against this view contemporary forms of
"anthropological theology" stress the positive relationship established in incarnation: Barth called it
"theoanthropology" to indicate the *tertium quid*
posited beside the classical dichotomy of divinity
and humanity. Berdyaev argued in similar vein, for a
positive "apprehension of the humanity, i.e. of the
divine humanity of God" beyond the negative apprehension of mystery (BERDYAEV: 46, 52f). Emil Brunner
maintains that scripture has no doctrine of God or of
man "in himself" (*Gott-an-sich, Menschen-an-sich*)
but only of God who approaches man and of man who
comes from God (*Gott-zum-Menschen-hin, Menschen-von-
Gott-her*). Indeed, "That God--even in His 'I-am-ness'
(*An-sich-Sein*)--wishes from the first to be understood

as the God who approaches man is precisely the meaning of the doctrine of the Triune God" (BRUNNER 1943: 46ff). Elsewhere Brunner asserts that "the Nameless One" of the classical tradition is *not* "the truly Mysterious One" who reveals his mystery through the Name, and accuses the Greek Fathers of turning the name of Yahweh into an ontological definition: "The 'Name' which cannot be defined is turned into a definition" (BRUNNER 1949: 119f).

The contemporary debate is more than a qualification of certain excesses in classical theism. The charge is not Harnack's "hellenization" but a somewhat different one which concerns the very choice of theological model and the trauma of shifting to alternative--or complementary--models. It resembles the Copernican revolution in cosmology, or the "paradigm shift" in modern science (WILES: 142f, 168ff). The Ptolemaic world-view had become so complex because of the numerous qualifications (epicycle on epicycle) added to meet new data and changing thought-forms that the simplicity and elegance of the Copernican model offered a clear alternative. On this analogy, the traditional doctrine of God rooted in classical thinking has become so complex through the qualifications added by its defenders that it is unstable and ready to give way to a more elegant alternative. It is one thing to say of the *via negationis* that "It knows better than by concepts that very thing in which the conceptual formulae of dogma communicate to human understanding" (MARITAIN: 12); but such defence of classical apophasis begs the question. For it, Spinoza's dictum still holds true, *Omnis determinatio est negatio*.

What theology needs to learn today is that the traditional "theory of the concept" fails to appreciate the creative role of *language* itself in establishing human being. Or better, to borrow Gabriel Marcel's approach: a phenomenology of "presence" is required in which the distinction between problem and mystery will be honored but in which the role of

imagination, the "esthetic" domain so to speak, will
be allowed its play through and beyond the dialectic
of reason. The modern style of aphoristic and explora-
tory theology reflects this approach. To be sure, none
of this is quite missing from classical theism, in
which the *mysterion* symbolized a more than noetic or
metaphysical inquiry. Yet today one needs to "overcome
history by history" and to overcome theology by a doctrine of God that will function for modern man as well
as classical theism did for its age.

Our conclusion has but noted certain elements
in the theological project required in view of the
breakdown of classical theism. That it is a radical
project--a root change--is evident when one considers
the implications of contemporary theories of the epistemology involved in "the new philosophy" of language.
One influential philosopher in this respect is Michael
Polanyi, whose "post-critical" theory of knowledge
scores the classical ideal of "objectivity" on behalf
of that proper objectivity of "personal knowledge"
which accepts relational interaction as the key to
"truth;" indeed, "Objectivism has totally falsified
our conception of truth" (POLANYI: 286; cf 3ff).
Even those "philosophies of revolt" mentioned above--
positivism and existentialism--operate within "this
single conceptual frame" dictated by the ideal of objectivity (GRENE: 13). If Polanyi is correct, we need
to develop a "postlogical" instrument, a poetics which
will serve as "a choreography of language and mind"
under the sign of Orpheus (SEWELL: 34).

So long as we assume that truth is simply
adaequatio rei et intellectus, we assume with
Parmenides that language is merely outward expression
of inward thought, missing the fact that the word
shapes "reality" and communicates more than we think
(DEWART 1969: 57ff). Gabriel Marcel has stressed the
role of the creative imagination, the judgment of the
wordmaker, the poet (MARCEL: I.57ff). It is Paul
Ricoeur who has clarified the direction of a
"philosophy of the will" as the project of a hermeneutic of myths and symbols: "Le symbole donne à

penser" (cf RICOEUR: 347ff). Perhaps this development of French philosophy, in contrast to British neo-empiricism, results from the historical fact that Descartes had grasped the Parmenidean starting-point with a vengeance, underlining the significance of the *Cogito* as a problem in willing.

We began this essay by accusing the Alexandrians of selecting from the rich tradition of "Greek religion and philosophy" what was essentially the line of "optimistic rationalism" and so neglecting that "other Greece" which tested the weight of mystery and tragedy. There are many points, of course, at which the Alexandrians are more open to this otherness. For instance, their basis for the allegorical method is the insight into the hiddenness of truth, which requires a subtle hermeneutic to allow the text to "show" the truth it intends--a striking formal likeness to Ricoeur's project. Nor are we suggesting that the cure for optimistic rationalism is pessimistic irrationalism! Rather, our project is to explain the modalities of understanding by moving beyond the *problématique* of classical theism toward a *poétique* that will respect the heritage of "mystery and tragedy" as well. To continue the scheme of Ricoeur, this will involve as crucial phase the *pathétique* whose proper language is myth and rhetoric (e.g. RICOEUR: 3ff). To measure *pathos* in a way impossible for the Alexandrian world-view opens up new possibilities in terms of alternative ways of describing the human journey and of assessing the relationship between tragedy and comedy (McLELLAND 1970: 61ff).

One of the deepest insights of the poetic tradition has been to see that the phenomenon of *naming* has a deeper dimension than philosophers have thought. One sees this most clearly in the task which James Joyce set himself, the exploration of the "monomyth;" and in those poets so influential on modern philosophical theologians: Hölderlin and Rilke. Closer to home, it is expressed well by A.M. Klein,

176

for whom the artist is
        the nth Adam taking a green inventory
        in world but scarcely uttered, naming, praising..
            (*Portrait of the Artist as Landscape*)

We have suggested the superiority of the
modern "theoanthropology" over the dichotomy of classical theism. Yet to give a name to God is no easy
matter, nor can it escape the reverent caution of the
Alexandrian tradition. Charles Williams once remarked
of Origen that he was "suspected of a great orthodoxy."
To attend to the Alexandrian philosophical theology
for a little is to overhear a remarkable conversation
about the deepest of all questions. And to learn some
answers well worth the hearing; above all, to learn a
style, a human way that endures as one outstanding
example of a noble response to Mystery.

B I B L I O G R A P H Y

ALBRIGHT W.F.
  1940   *From Stone Age to Christianity*
                      Baltimore: Hopkins

ANGUS S.
  1925   *The Mystery-Religions and*
                      Christianity N.Y.: Scribners

ARMSTRONG A.H.
  1965   *An Introduction to Ancient*
                      Philosophy London: Methuen

  1967   ed. *The Cambridge History of*
                      Later Greek and Early Medieval
                      Philosophy Cambridge U.P.

ARMSTRONG A.H. and MARKUS R.A.
  1960   *Christian Faith and Greek*
                      Philosophy London: Darton,
                      Longman and Todd

ARNOU R.
  1933   'Platonisme des Pères,'
                      Dictionnaire de théol.
                      catholique XII, pp 2258-2392
                      Paris

BALTHASAR H. URS VON
  1938   *Origenes: Geist und Feuer*
                      Leipzig

  1957   *Parole et Mystère chez Origène*
                      Paris: Ed. de Cerf

179

BARDENHEWER O.
1962   *Geschichte der Altkirchlichen Literatur* Zweiter Band. Darmstadt

BARDY G.
1933   'Origène,' *Dictionnaire de théol. cath.* XI, pp 1489-1565 Paris

BARNARD L.W.
1972   *Athenagoras* Paris: Beauchesne

BARTH K.
1936-1969   *Church Dogmatics,* 13 vols. Edinburgh: T & T Clark

BERDYAEV N.
1953   *Truth and Revelation* London: Geoffrey Bles

BIENERT W.A.
1972   *'Allegoria' und 'Anagoge' bei Didymos dem Blinden von Alexandria* Berlin: Walter de Gruyter

BIGG C.
1886   *The Christian Platonists of Alexandria* Oxford: Clarendon

BLAKNEY R.B.
1941   *Meister Eckhart: a modern translation* N.Y.: Harper

BONHOEFFER D.
1959   *Creation and Fall* London: SCM

BOUYER L.
1963   *A History of Christian Spiritua-*
lity, I: The Spirituality of the
N.T. and the Fathers
London: Burns and Oates

BREHIER E.
1908   *Les Idées Philosophiques et*
Religieuses de Philon d'Alexandrie
Paris

BRUNNER E.
1944   *Divine-Human Encounter*
London: SCM

1949   *The Christian Doctrine of God*
(Dogmatics I) London: Lutterworth

BUBER M.
1946   *Moses* Oxford: East and West
Library

BURI F.
1939   *Clemens Alexandrinus und der*
Paulinische Freiheitsbegriff
Zürich and Leipzig

BUTTERWORTH G.W.
1915-1916   'The deification of man in Clement
of Alexandria' *JTS* 17: 157-169

CADIOU R.
1932   *Introduction au système d'Origène*
Paris

1935   *La Jeunesse d'Origène*
Paris

CAIRD E.
    1904   *The Evolution of Theology in the*
                     Greek Philosophers, 2 vols.
                     Glasgow

CALLAHAN J.F.
    1967   *Augustine and the Greek*
                     Philosophers Villanova U.P.

CAMELOT P.Th.
    1945   *Foi et Gnose: Introduction à*
                     l'Etude de la Connaissance
                     Mystique chez Clément d'Alexandrie
                     Paris: Lib. Phil. J. Vrin

CASEY R.P.
    1925   'Clement of Alexandria and the
                     beginnings of Christian Platonism,"
                     HTR 18: 39-101

CHADWICK H.
    1965   *Origen: Contra Celsum*
                     translated with introduction and
                     notes Cambridge U.P.

    1966   *Early Christian Thought and the*
                     Classical Tradition
                     Oxford: Clarendon Press

    1967   'Philo and the Beginnings of
                     Christian Thought,' *The Cambridge*
                     History of Later Greek and Early
                     Medieval Philosophy,
                     ed. A.H. Armstrong Cambridge U.P.

CHADWICK O.
    1950   *John Cassian: a study in*
                     primitive monasticism
                     Cambridge U.P.

COCHRANE C.N.
1944   *Christianity and Classical
               Culture* Oxford U.P.

COPLESTON F.C.
1946   *A History of Philosophy*, 7 vols.
               Doubleday Image

CORNFORD F.M.
1935   *Plato's Theory of Knowledge*
               London: Kegan Paul

1939   *Plato and Parmenides*
               London: Kegan Paul

1957   *From Religion to Philosophy*
               N.Y.: Harper

1961   *The Origin of Attic Comedy*
               N.Y.: Doubleday

COX H.
1965   *The Secular City*
               N.Y.: Macmillan

CROMBIE I.M.
1963   *An Examination of Plato's
               Doctrines*, 2 vols. London:
               Routledge and Kegan Paul

CROUZEL H.
1956   *Théologie de l'Image de Dieu
               chez Origène* Paris: Aubier

1961   *Origène et la 'Connaissance
               Mystique'* Museum Lessianum,
               Bruges-Paris

1962   *Origène et la Philosophie*
               Paris: Aubier

DANIELOU J.
1944   *Platonisme et Théologie Mystique: essai sur la doctrine spirituelle de Saint Grégoire de Nysse*
Paris: Aubier

1955   *Origen* (trans. W. Mitchell)
N.Y.: Sheed and Ward

1960   *From Shadows to Reality*
(E.T. of *Sacramentum Futuri*)
London: Burns and Oates

1961   *Message évangélique et culture hellénistique*
Tournai: Desclée et Cie

1964   *The Theology of Jewish Christianity*
(trans. J.A. Baker) London

DANIELOU J. and MARROU H.
1964   *The Christian Centuries, Vol. I: The First Six Hundred Years*
London: Darton, Longman & Todd

DAVIES W.D.
1948   *Paul and Rabbinic Judaism*
London: SPCK

DE LUBAC H.
1950   *Histoire et Esprit: l'Intelligence de l'écriture d'après Origène* Paris: Aubier

1951   *Aspects du Bouddhisme*
Paris: Ed du Seuil

DE FAYE E.
1906   *Clément d'Alexandrie* Paris

DE FAYE E.
    1925   *Esquisse de la pensée d'Origène*
                              Paris

    1926   *Origen and his work*
                              London: Allen and Unwin

DEWART L.
    1966   *The Future of Belief*
                              N.Y.: Herder and Herder

    1969   *The Foundations of Belief*
                              N.Y.: Herder and Herder

DODD C.H.
    1953   *The Interpretation of the Fourth Gospel* Cambridge

DODDS E.R.
    1933   ed., *Proclus: The Elements of Theology* Oxford

    1951   *The Greeks and the Irrational*
                              Berkeley: U. of Cal. Press

DODS M.
    1891   'Clement of Alexandria and his Apologetic,' *Erasmus and Other Essays*
                            London: Hodder and Stoughton

DREWERY B.
    1960   *Origen and the doctrine of grace*
                            London: Epworth Press

DRUMMOND J.
    1969   *Philo Judaeus or the Jewish-Alexandrian Philosophy*
                            Amsterdam: Philo Press
                          (reprint of 1888 edition)

185

DUMERY H.
    1964   *The Problem of God in Philosophy
                        of Religion* (trans. C. Courtney)
                        Northwestern U.P.

ELERT W.
    1957   *Der Ausgang der altkirchlichen
                        Christologie* Berlin

FAIRBAIRN A.M.
    1907   *The Place of Christ in Modern
                        Theology* N.Y.: Scribners

FESTUGIERE R.P.
    1944-1954   *La Révélation d'Hermès Trismégiste,*
                        4 vols. Paris

FLOYD W.E.G.
    1971   *Clement of Alexandria's treatment
                        of the problem of evil*
                        London: O.U.P.

FRIEDLANDER P.
    1964   *Plato, an Introduction*
                        N.Y.: Harper

GILKEY L.
    1969   *Naming the Whirlwind: the Renewal
                        of God-Language*
                        N.Y.: Bobbs-Merrill

GILSON E.
    1955   *History of Christian Philosophy
                        in the Middle Ages*
                        N.Y.: Random House

186

GOLDMANN L.
    1964   *The Hidden God: a study of tragic vision in the Pensées of Pascal and the tragedies of Racine*
                        London: Routledge and Kegan Paul

GOODENOUGH E.R.
    1935   *By Light, Light; the mystical Gospel of Hellenistic Judaism*
                        New Haven: Yale U.P.

    1940   *An Introduction to Philo Judaeus*
                        New Haven: Yale U.P.

GRANT F.C.
    1953   ed., *Hellenistic Religions*
                        N.Y.: Bobbs Merrill

GRANT R.M.
    1957   *The Letter and the Spirit*
                        London: SPCK

    1959   *Gnosticism and Early Christianity*
                        N.Y.: Columbia U.P.

    1961   *Gnosticism: an Anthology*
                        London: Collins

    1966   *The Early Christian Doctrine of God* Charlottesville: U. of Virginia

    1967   *After the New Testament*
                        Phila.: Fortress

GRENE M.
    1966   *The Knower and the Known*
                        London: Faber and Faber

GRILLMEIER A.
1965   *Christ in Christian Tradition*
(trans. Jas. Bowden)
N.Y.:   Sheed and Ward

GUTTMANN L.
1964   *Philosophies of Judaism*
N.Y.:   Holt, Rinehart & Winston

HARL M.
1958   *Origène et la Fonction Révélatrice
du Verbe Incarné*
Paris: ed. du Seuil

HANSON R.P.C.
1954   *Origen's Doctrine of Tradition*
London: SPCK

1959   *Allegory and Event: a study of
the sources and significance of
Origen's interpretation of
scripture*
Richmond: John Knox Press

HARNACK A. VON
1957   *What is Christianity?*
N.Y.:   Harper
(E.T. of 1900 edition)

1961   *History of Dogma*,   7 vols.
N.Y.:   Dover
(E.T. of 3rd ed. ca 1900)

1962   *The Mission and Expansion of
Christianity*
N.Y.:   Harper
(E.T. of 1908 edition)

HARRISON J.
    1955   *Prolegomena to the study of*
                    Greek religion   N.Y.: Meridian

HARTSHORNE C.
    1948   *The Divine Relativity: a social*
                    conception of God   Yale U.P.

HARTSHORNE C. and REESE W.L.
    1953   *Philosophers Speak of God*
                    Chicago U.P.

HATCH E.
    1957   *The Influence of Greek Ideas*
                    on Christianity   N.Y.: Harper

HEIDEGGER M.
    1947   *Platons Lehre von der Wahrheit*
                    Bern: A. Francke

    1962   *Being and Time*
                    (trans. J. Macquarrie and
                    E. Robinson) London: SCM

HENRY P.
                    'The Place of Plotinus in the
                    History of Thought'   intro. to
                    Plotinus: the Enneads
                    McKenna-Page ed. xxxv-lxx (n.d.)

HERING J.
    1923   *Etude sur la doctrine de la chute*
                    et de la préexistence des âmes
                    chez Clément d'Alexandrie   Paris

HICK J.
    1966   *Evil and the God of Love*
                    London: Macmillan

HORT F.J.A. and MAYOR J.B.
    1902   *Clement of Alexandria,*
                          Miscellanies Bk VII
                          London: Macmillan

HUGEL F. VON
    1921   'Suffering and God' in *Essays*
                          and Addresses on the Philosophy
                          of Religion London: J.M. Dent

INGE W.R.
    1946   *Origen* Proceedings of the
                          British Academy

JAEGER W.
    1934   *Aristotle* Oxford:
                          Clarendon Press

    1945   *Paideia: the Ideals of Greek*
                          Culture, 3 vols. N.Y.: O.U.P.

    1947   *The Theology of the Early Greek*
                          Philosophers Oxford

    1954   *Two Rediscovered Works of ancient*
                          Christian literature: Gregory of
                          Nyssa and Macarius
                          Leiden: E.J. Brill

    1961   *Early Christianity and Greek*
                          Paideia Harvard U.P.

JAMES E.O.
    1935   *The Old Testament in the Light*
                          of Anthropology London: SPCK

    1958   *Myth and Ritual in the Ancient*
                          Near East London

JAY E.G.
    1954   *Origen's Treatise on Prayer*
                   London: SPCK

JONAS H.
    1963   *The Gnostic Religion: the message
                 of the Alien God and the begin-
                 nings of Christianity*
                 Boston: Beacon Press

JOWETT B.
    1924   *The Dialogues of Plato*, 5 vols.
                 Oxford (3rd ed.)

KAUFMANN W.
    1961   *Critique of Religion and
                 Philosophy*
                 N.Y.: Doubleday Anchor Books

KELLY J.N.D.
    1958   *Early Christian Doctrines*
                 London: A and C Black

KENNEDY H.A.A.
    1919   *Philo's Contribution to Religion*
                 London: Hodder and Stoughton

KERENYI C.
    1967   *Eleusis: archetypal image of
                 Mother and Daughter*
                 N.Y.: Bollingen Series LXV.4

KERR H.T.
    1958   *The first systematic theologian,
                 Origen of Alexandria*
                 Princeton Pamphlets 11

KIERKEGAARD S.
1966   *The Concept of Irony with*
   constant reference to Socrates
   London: Collins (1841 thesis)

KIRK G.S. and RAVEN J.E.
1957   *The Presocratic Philosophers*
   Cambridge U.P.

KIRK K.E.
1931   *The Vision of God*
   London: Longmans, Green

KITAMORI K.
1965   *Theology of the Pain of God*
   Richmond: John Knox Press

KLIBANSKY R.
1939   *The Continuity of the Platonic*
   Tradition during the middle ages:
   outlines of a Corpus Platonicum
   Medii Aevi London: Warburg Inst.

KOCH H.
1932   *Pronoia und Paideusis: studien*
   über Origenes und sein Verhältnis
   zum Platonismus Leipzig

KRONER R.
1956   *Speculation in Pre-Christian*
   Philosophy Phila.: Westminster

1959   *Speculation and Revelation in the*
   Age of Christian Philosophy
   Phila.: Westminster

LAPORTE J.
1972   *La Doctrine Eucharistique chez*
   Philon d'Alexandrie
   Paris: Beauchesne

LEE J.Y.
    1974   *God Suffers For Us*
                        The Hague: M. Nijhoff

LIESKE P.A.
    1938   *Die Theologie der Logosmystik*
                        bei Origenes Münster

LILLA S.R.
    1971   *Clement of Alexandria: a study*
                        in Christian Platonism and
                        Gnosticism London: O.U.P.

LONERGAN B.
    1967   'The Dehellenization of Dogma'
                        in *The Future of Belief Debate,*
                        ed. G. Baum N.Y.: Herder and Herder

LOSSKY V.
    1957   *The Mystical Theology of the*
                        Eastern Church London: Jas Clarke

    1960   *Théologie Négative et Connaissance*
                        de Dieu chez Maître Eckhart
                        Paris: Lib. Phil. J. Vrin

MACGREGOR G.H.C. and PURDY A.C.
    1936   *Jew and Greek: tutors unto Christ*
                        London

MANSI J.D.
    1901   *Sacrorum Conciliorum,* 42 vols.
                        Paris

MARCEL G.
    1950-1951   *The Mystery of Being,* 2 vols.
                        London: Harvill Press

MARITAIN J.
1959

Distinguish to Unite, or the
Degrees of Knowledge (trans.
Gerald Phelan) N.Y.: Scribners

MARSH H.G.
1936

'The Use of Μυστήριον in the
writings of Clement of Alexandria
with special reference to his
sacramental doctrine,'
JTS 37: 64-80

McLELLAND J.C.
1957

The Visible Words of God: the
sacramental theology of Peter
Martyr Vermigli
Edinburgh: Oliver and Boyd

1965

'Calvin and Philosophy,'
The Canadian Journal of Theology
XI.1: 42-53

1968

'The Alexandrian Quest of the
Non-historical Christ,'
Church History XXXVII.4: 355-364

1970

The Clown and the Crocodile
Richmond: John Knox Press

1974

'Philosophy and Theology--a Family
Affair (Karl and Heinrich Barth)'
M. Rumscheidt, ed., Footnotes to
a Theology: the Karl Barth
Colloquium of 1972, 30-52
Waterloo, Ont.

MEHAT A.
1966

Etude sur les 'Stromates' de
Clément d'Alexandrie
Paris: ed. du Seuil

MEIFORT J.
1928   *Der Platonismus bei Clemens
                Alexandrinus* Tübingen

MEIJERING E.P.
1968   *Orthodoxy and Platonism in
                Athanasius* Leiden: E.J. Brill

MERKI H.
1952   ʿΟΜΟΙΩΣΙΣ ΘΕΩ *Von der Platonischen
                Angleichung an Gott zur Gottähnlich-
                keit bei Gregor von Nyssa*
                Freiburg 1952 (Paradosis VII)

MERLAN P.
1953   *From Platonism to Neoplatonism*
                The Hague: M. Nijhoff

1967   'Greek Philosophy from Plato to
                Plotinus', *The Cambridge History
                of Later Greek and Early Medieval
                Philosophy*, ed. A.H. Armstrong
                pp 14-132 Cambridge U.P.

MEYENDORFF J.
1969   *Christ in Eastern Christian
                Thought* Washington: Corpus Books

MEYENDORFF J. and McLELLAND J.C.
1973   *The New Man: an Orthodox and
                Reformed dialogue*
                New Brunswick, N.J.: Agora Books

MIURA-STANGE A.
1926   *Celsus und Origenes: das
                Gemeinsame ihrer Weltanschauung*
                Giessen

MOLLAND E.
 1938   *The Conception of the Gospel in
              the Alexandrian Theology* Oslo

 1970   *Opuscula Patristica* Oslo

MOLTMANN J.
 1974   *The Crucified God* London: SCM

MONDESERT C.
 1944   *Clément d'Alexandrie. Introduction
              à l'étude de sa pensée religieuse
              à partir de l'Ecriture* Paris

MOZLEY J.K.
 1926   *The Impassibility of God*
              Cambridge U.P.

MURRAY G.
 1912   'Excursus on the ritual forms
              preserved in Greek Tragedy,' in
              J. Harrison, *Themis* Cambridge U.P.

 1946   *Stoic, Christian and Humanist*
              London: Geo. Allen and Unwin

 1953   *Hellenism and the Modern World*
              London: Geo. Allen and Unwin

NIEBUHR H.R.
 1951   *Christ and Culture*
              N.Y.: Harper and Bros.

NILSSON M.P.
 1948   *Greek Piety* (trans. H.J. Rose)
              Oxford: Clarendon Press

NOCK A.D.
    1933   *Conversion: the Old and the New in Religion from Alexander the Great to Augustine of Hippo* Oxford: Clarendon Press

NOCK A.D. and FESTUGIERE R.P.
    1945   *Corpus Hermeticum,* 4 vols. Paris

NORDEN E.
    1913   *Agnostos Theos* Leipzig-Berlin

NORRIS R.A.
    1965   *God and World in Early Christian Theology* N.Y.: Seabury

NYGREN A.
    1953   *Agape and Eros* (trans. P.S. Watson) London: SPCK

OSBORN E.F.
    1957   *The Philosophy of Clement of Alexandria* Cambridge U.P.

OULTON J.E.L. and CHADWICK H.
    1954   *Alexandrian Christianity* LCC vol. II. London SCM

PANNENBERG W.
    1971   'The Appropriation of the philosophical concept of God as a dogmatic problem of Early Christian Theology,' *Basic Questions in Theology* Phila.: Fortress

PATTERSON L.G.
    1966   *God and History in Early Christian Thought* N.Y.: Seabury

PELIKAN J.
1962   *The Light of the World*
N.Y.: Harper and Bros.

1966   *The Finality of Jesus Christ in an Age of Universal History*
Richmond: John Knox Press

1969   *Development of Christian Doctrine*
Yale U.P.

1971   *The Christian Tradition, I: The emergence of the Catholic tradition (100-600)*
U. of Chicago Press

PEPIN J.
1961   *Les Deux Approches du Christianisme*
Paris

PETREMENT S.
1947   *Le Dualisme chez Platon, les Gnostiques et les Manichéens*
Paris: Presses U. de France

PETTAZZONI R.
1953   *La Religion dans la Grèce Antique*
(trans. J. Gouillard) Paris

PLOTINUS   *The Enneads* (trans. S. Mackenna and B.S. Page) N.Y.: Pantheon
(n.d.)

POHLENZ M.
1943   *Klemens von Alexandreia und sein hellenisches Christentum*
Göttingen

POLANYI M.
1958   *Personal Knowledge: towards a*
                post-critical philosophy
                N.Y.: Harper and Row

POLLARD T.E.
1955   'The Impassibility of God'
                in *SJT* Dec. 1955, 353–364

PRESTIGE G.L.
1958   *Fathers and Heretics*
                London: SPCK

QUASTEN J.
1950–1960   *Patrology*, 3 vols.
                Spectrum/Newman

RAHNER K.
1970   *The Trinity*
                N.Y.: Herder and Herder

REITZENSTEIN R.
1956   *Die hellenistischen Mysterien-*
                religionen nach ihren Grundgedanken
                und Wirkungen Stuttgart

RICHARDSON H.
1967   *Toward an American Theology*
                N.Y.: Harper and Row

RICOEUR P.
1969   *The Symbolism of Evil*
                Boston: Beacon Press

RITSCHL D.
1964   *Athanasius: Versuch einer*
                Interpretation Theol. Studien 76
                Zürich

ROBINSON H.W.
1955   *The Cross in the Old Testament*
                London: SCM

ROLT C.E.
1920   *Dionysius the Areopagite on the Divine Names and the Mystical Theology* London: SPCK

ROSE H.J.
1958   'Divine Names in Classical Greece' *HTR* LI.I (January 1958) pp 3-38

RUSSELL B.
1961   *History of Western Philosophy* London: Geo. Allen and Unwin

SCOTT W.
1924   ed., *Hermetica*, 3 vols. Oxford U.P.

SELLERS R.V.
1954   *Two Ancient Christologies* London: SPCK

SEWELL E.
1971   *The Orphic Voice: Poetry and Natural History* N.Y.: Harper and Row

SHAPLAND C.R.B.
1951   *The Letters of St. Athanasius Concerning the Holy Spirit* London: Epworth

SHIDELER M.M.
1962   *The Theology of Romantic Love: a study in the writings of Charles Williams* Grand Rapids: Eerdmans

SPANNEUT M.
1957   *Le Stoïcisme des Pères de l'Eglise de Clément de Rome à Clément d'Alexandrie* Paris: Ed. du Seuil

STAHMER H.
1968   *Speak That I may See Thee*
                N.Y.: Macmillan

TAYLOR A.E.
1949   *Plato, the Man and his Work*
                London: Methuen 6th ed.

TILLICH P.
1951–1963   *Systematic Theology*, 3 vols.
                Chicago: U. of Chicago Press

TOLLINTON R.B.
1914   *Clement of Alexandria*, 2 vols.
                London

1929   *Selections from the Commentaries
                and Homilies of Origen*
                London: SPCK

1932   *Alexandrine Teaching on the
                Universe* London

TORRANCE T.F.
1948   *The Doctrine of Grace in the
                Apostolic Fathers*
                Edinburgh: Oliver and Boyd

1965   *Theology in Reconstruction*
                London: SCM

1966   'The Implications of Oikonomia for
                Knowledge and Speech of God in
                Early Christian Theology,'
                *Oikonomia: Heilsgeschichte als
                Thema den Theologie*
                Hamburg: Herbert Reich Evang.
                Verlag

VOLKER W.
1931   *Das Volkommenheitsideal des Origenes* Tübingen

1952   *Der Wahre Gnostiker nach Clemens Alexandrinus* Berlin

WAGNER W.H.
1971   'A Father's Fate; attitudes toward and interpretations of Clement of Alexandria,' *Journal of Religious History* 6/3, 209-231

WALKER D.P.
1972   *The Ancient Theology: studies in Christian Platonism from the fifteenth to the eighteenth century* Ithaca, N.Y.: Cornell U.P.

WATMOUGH J.R.
1934   *Orphism* Cambridge U.P.

WEIL S.
1957   *Intimations of Christianity among the ancient Greeks* London: Routledge and Kegan Paul

WESTCOTT B.F.
1887   'Origenes,' *A Dictionary of Christian Biography*, ed. Smith and Wace, Vol. 4, 96-142 London

WHEELWRIGHT P.
1959   *Heraclitus* Princeton U.P.

WHITEHEAD A.N.
1929   *Process and Reality* N.Y.: Macmillan

1933   *Adventures of Ideas* N.Y.: Macmillan

WILES M.
    1967   *The Making of Christian Doctrine* Cambridge

WILSON R.McL.
    1958   *The Gnostic Problem* London: Mowbray

WINDELBAND W.
    1958   *History of Philosophy*, 2 vols. N.Y.: Harper

WITT R.E.
    1931   'The Hellenism of Clement of Alexandria,' *Classical Quarterly* 25

    1937   *Albinus and the History of Middle Platonism* Cambridge

WOLFSON H.A.
    1947   *Philo: foundations of religious philosophy in Judaism, Christianity and Islam*, 2 vols. Harvard U.P.

    1952   'Albinus and Plotinus on Divine Attributes,' *HTR* 45

    1956   *The Philosophy of the Church Fathers (Vol. 1: Faith, Trinity, Incarnation)* Harvard U.P.

    1957   'Negative Attributes in the Church Fathers and the Gnostic Basilides,' *HTR* 50.3

    1964   'Notes on Patristic Philosophy,' *HTR* 57.2

    1965   *Religious Philosophy: a group of essays* N.Y.: Atheneum

ZELLER E.
    1888   *Plato and the Older Academy* London

Calvin   169
Cappadocians   145ff
Cassian, John   126
Celsus   95ff
Chadwick H.   26f, 29, 96
Chadwick O.   159
Chalcedon   157
Chrysostom   149ff
CLEMENT   *45ff*; works 48ff; on: christology 67ff;
            faith 54ff; knowledge 83ff;
            logos 64ff; method 60ff; mysticism
            50, 78ff; philosophy 50ff
Constantinople (Second)   121, 159

Daniélou J.   96, 129, 168
Denis (Areopagite)   126, 152ff
Dewart L.   170f
dialectic   54ff
Dionysos   5, 8, 51
Docetism   75ff

Eckhart   150, 155f
ecstasy   40ff, 129f; see mysticism
Eleusis   6, 49
Eliot T.S.   95
encyclia   61, 84, 96
enhypostasia   158
epinoiai   101, 107, 110, 119ff
epopteia   4, 55
Euclid   17, 62
eudaimonia   79f
Eunomius   147ff
eupatheia   43
Eusebius   45, 47f, 95, 97
Evagrius   126, 159

Festugière   20, 36
Freidländer   8f, 12

Gilson   60, 168
gnôsis   54ff, 85ff
Gnosticism   23f, 65, 72f, 93, 151f
Goodenough, E.R.   31, 44
Gregory Nazianzus   145f
Gregory of Nyssa   146f
Gregory Thaumaturgus   96, 141ff

Harnack   iv, 14, 93, 106
Harrison, Jane   3f
Hartshorne, C.   163f
Heidegger   1
Hellenization   93, 97, 170
Heraclitus   27ff
Hermetica   23, 151f
historia   112ff, 148
homoousios   82, 101, 143

Ignatius   124f, 151
impassibility   37ff, 67ff, 83, 147
immutability   37ff, 64, 69, 83, 106, 146f
incarnation   71ff, 107ff, 147
incomprehensibility of God   33, 64, 100, 147ff;
                of *ousia*   37, 103, 149

Jaeger W.   8, 138
John of Damascus   154f
Justin Martyr   45f

Kant   162
Kerenyi C.   4
Kitamori K.   164f
Klibansky R.   98, 140
Koch H.   93

Lilla S.   20, 50
logos   11ff, 23ff, 64ff, 80, 100ff, 147
Lossky V.   129, 156

Rahner K.   172
Richardson H.   159
Ricoeur P.   v, 7, 176
Rosenzweig F.   163, 167

Septuagint   25f
Socrates   2, 10f
Stoicism   27f, 30

Tertullian   54
Tetragrammaton   25f, 34, 167f
Thales   8
theōria   89, 94, 97, 100, 128, 139, 148
theōsis   87f, 112f, 127
Therapeutae   30
Tillich P.   164
Torrance T.F.   25, 55
tragedy   4ff, 91, 176
Transfiguration   119ff, 129

unio hypostatica   141, 158

Valentinus   24, 66, 76, 114
via triplex   17ff, 104, 139
Völker W.   40

Whitehead   7, 164
Williams C.   160, 177
wisdom   23ff, 110f
Wolfson H.   17, 20, 26, 35f, 139

Zeus   v, 3